Religious Philosophy and

Ult *Tuson* *s*

GCSE

Lesle

HODDER
EDUCATION
AN HACHETTE UK COMPANY

Acknowledgements

My first thanks have to go to Diana Hayden, without whose inspired teaching I wouldn't even have got to try out this subject. It's probably her fault I'm an RE teacher! I hope those studying the course get the same sense of wanting to know and pick apart ideas – whether through curiosity or devilment! Thanks to Debbie Garnett for the faith shown in me to let me work as part of the Specification Development team at AQA, from which came this new specification. Also for letting me run with my spec suggestions – from which came three new courses, all of which I am very proud. Thanks to Jim Belben and Hodder for continuing to give me the opportunities to write in my style, and to get these books out. Thanks to the teachers for making Hodder want to give me those chances. Oscar speech over! Enjoy the book.

Photo credits

The Publishers would like to thank the following for permission to reproduce copyright material:

Cover © Tony Arruza/Corbis; **p.2** Corbis/Jose Luis Pelaez, Inc; **p.4** *t* Science Photo Library/Ed Young, *ct* NASA, *cb* Alamy/Scott Camazine, *b* Purestock X; **p.6** *tl* Gett Images/Hola Images, *tc* www.theboltonnews.co.uk, *tr* PA Photos/ Fernado Antonia/AP, *bl* Still Pictures/Dominic Sansoni/Majority World, *bc* PA Photos/Charles Rex Arbogast/AP, *br* PA Photos/Scott Heppell; **p.7** *t* © Lesley Parry, *b* Corbis/Reuters; **p.8** *t* Corbis/Stefano Bianchetti, *b* Photodisc/Getty Images; **p.11** *t* Corbis/Jacques Pavlovsky/Sygma, *ct* PA Photos/Haraz N. Ghanbarid/AP, *c* Getty Images/Alex Livesey, *cb* Alamy/Stuart Abraham, *b* Alamy Gavin Hellier; **p.21** Science Photo Library/Mehau Kulyk; **p.22** Corbis/Philip Gould; **p.23** *t* Alamy/Steve Skjold, *b* Corbis/Arne Hodalic; **p.24** Rex Features; **p.25** *t* PA Photos/Charles Kelly/AP, *b* PA Photos/ Bebeto Matthews/AP; **p.32** *t* Corbis/Alinari Archives, *b* Alamy/Mary Evans Picture Library; **p.34** *tl* Corbis/Andy Rain/ EPA, *tr* Alamy/VStock, *bl* Rex Features/Sipa Press, *br* Corbis/Kim Ritzenthaler/Dallas Morning News; **p.52** *both* © Lesley Parry; **p.59** © Lesley Parry; **p.61** *l* Rex Features/Paul Cooper, *r* Corbis/Arko Datta/Reuters; **p.62** *t* Corbis/Matthew Polak/Sygma, *b* Getty Images/Time & Life Pictures; **p.71** Purestock X; **p.74** *all* Stockbyte/Getty Images; **p.78** Alamy/ Pictorial Press Ltd; **p.79** Corbis/Bettmann; **p.80** *t* Alamy/INTERFOTO Pressebildagentur, *tc* Corbis/Stapleton Collection, *c* Corbis/Bettmann, *bc* Alamy/Pictorial Press Ltd, *b* Corbis/Bettmann; **p.81** *l* Alamy/Amoret Tanner, *r* Photodisc/Getty Images; **p.82** *tr* Alamy/North Wind Picture Archives, *cl* Alamy/Juniors Bildarchive, *cr* Alamy/David J Slater, *b* Corbis/Paul Vicente/EPA; **p.95** © Lesley Parry

Every effort has been made to trace all copyright holders, but if any have been inadvertently overlooked the Publishers will be pleased to make the necessary arrangements at the first opportunity.

Words highlighted in **bold** are defined in the Glossary on p.98.

Although every effort has been made to ensure that website addresses are correct at time of going to press, Hodder Education cannot be held responsible for the content of any website mentioned in this book. It is sometimes possible to find a relocated web page by typing in the address of the home page for a website in the URL window of your browser.

Hachette UK's policy is to use papers that are natural, renewable and recyclable products and made from wood grown in sustainable forests. The logging and manufacturing processes are expected to conform to the environmental regulations of the country of origin.

Orders: please contact Bookpoint Ltd, 130 Milton Park, Abingdon, Oxon OX14 4SB. Telephone: +44 (0)1235 827720. Fax: +44 (0)1235 400454. Lines are open 9.00–5.00, Monday to Saturday, with a 24-hour message answering service. Visit our website at www.hoddereducation.co.uk.

© Lesley Parry 2009
First published in 2009 by
Hodder Education,
An Hachette UK Company
338 Euston Road
London NW1 3BH

Impression number   5 4 3 2 1
Year   2013 2012 2011 2010 2009

Illustrations by Oxford Designers and Illustrators, Richard Duszczak.
Typeset in 11 point Minion by DC Graphic Design Limited, Swanley, Kent.
Printed in Italy
A catalogue record for this title is available from the British Library.

ISBN 978 0 340 98364 5

Contents

Introduction

This book has been written specifically to meet the AQA Specification B Unit 4 syllabus. It follows the Unit outline, moving through the topics in the order of the Unit as set out in the specification. It is informed additionally by the specification from which it grew (also called Specification B).

The Unit is examined through one exam paper of 1 hour and 30 minutes. All six topics within the Unit will be represented on that paper, though candidates will be required to answer questions on only four topics. Each question being worth 18 marks, and with quality of written response now within the mark scheme itself (rather than an additional sum), the total for the paper will be 72 marks. An example of the exam paper and what it should look like is found in Appendix II at the back of this book. This is annotated to help demystify the exam language and paper style.

Unit 4, when studied in conjunction with a second Unit, leads to a full GCSE qualification.

The topics within the book cover the Unit content from a variety of angles, as well as providing the necessary information required by those studying for the exam. Each topic asks students to think about what they are being told, and about the implications of the issues. There are many opportunities for evaluation work, which now forms 50 per cent of the total mark for the exam. Knowledge and understanding of the topics are important, but ability to apply that knowledge is vital to achieve the highest grades. The style of text is designed to encourage and develop exactly that.

Exam technique is a constant theme, as it can cost candidates many marks if poor. It is worth using class time to teach/learn good techniques via the mechanics of good answers. The author of this book is a Senior Examiner with AQA, and wrote the specification for AQA. This book gives valuable advice, so make good use of it!

Philosophy of religion has traditionally been studied in the Judaeo–Christian context. However, philosophy is not about specific religions, rather it is about concepts. This book deals with the concepts and encourages pupils to think around them. Much does relate to ideas coming from a Judaeo–Christian base. It is a stepping stone to AS level, and seeks to cover similar topics but at GCSE level.

Students should be encouraged to collect their own examples of the ideas as met in the news. They can collect, add comments and give their own opinion. This will help with their recall and provide real examples to call on in the exam.

A revision outline in Appendix I is designed to support revision, but can act as a checklist for students as they move through the course.

Can we prove God exists?

When you have heard people say they 'believe in God', what do they mean? Is it that they believe God will do something for them, or that God started some religions, or what? Or is it really that they believe in God's existence? You see to 'believe in' God doing anything, means you believe God exists in the first place, so what people are saying is that they *believe God exists*. Not everyone believes God exists – check your class out! So, what is it that has proved God's existence to some people, and not to everyone? Any ideas?

> If you think about it, every society has the same idea of right and wrong, so it must come from one source – God.

> God started off the world and everything – it can't have been an accident.

> I have met God.

> My dad recovered from an illness doctors said would definitely kill him – God helped.

> So beautiful is the world, it must have been planned – by God.

These statements are reasons why people believe in God. Of course, people believe because their parents, or some other significant person, told them that God exists, or they believe what it says in a holy book. However, these reasons aren't really useful to us as **proofs**. This course wants to know the 'proofs' of God's existence – and whether or not these really are proofs.

The 'proofs' we are going to look at are summed up in those five statements listed earlier. Read the following and see if you can spot which is which:

- **First Cause** argument.
- **Design** argument.
- Argument from **miracles**.
- Argument from **religious experience**.
- Argument from **morality**.

Well done! We are going to find out a bit more about each in this unit.

Oh yes, apart from saying what is wrong with the arguments, we need to look at why people *don't* believe that God exists – and that can be persuasive too! We'll get to that later.

Finally, these aren't the only arguments for God's existence – but they are the only ones on this course!

Exam Tips

For the exam, you might need to know: what the argument says; whose argument it is (because that helps you understand the way people thought); what is good about the argument (its strengths), and what is bad about it (its weaknesses). Some of the arguments are pretty persuasive – they must be because of how many people accept them as right.

The Basics

1 Can you think of some reasons why people believe that God exists?
2 Can you think of some reasons why people believe that God does not exist?
3 What are the five types of arguments for God's existence that the course covers?
4 Write a simple explanation of each type of argument. You could use the statements to help you.

The First Cause argument

Person Profile

St Thomas Aquinas was a Christian monk who lived from 1225–74CE. He wrote several books, including *Summa Theologica*, which gave his proofs of God's existence. He spoke of five different proofs. The second is about God being the Uncaused Cause, the First Cause of everything else. So, according to Aquinas – using the steps of the argument on this page – God was the cause of the universe. Now Aquinas, being a monk, could be accused of bias – of course his solution would be God, it's his job to say that!

Aquinas' argument

Step 1

Let's use the idea of the dominoes. Why do they fall? If nothing pushes them or acts on them to make them fall, will they ever fall? Now, think about the world around you and all the things in it. What causes each thing? Can you think of anything that is not caused by something else? Anything that is totally independent, not relying on something else for its existence?

Step 2

Bet you couldn't. It seems that everything relies on something else so that it can exist, or be. For example, that row of dominoes doesn't just fall over – something has to make the first domino move, so that the whole chain of dominoes falls in a sequence. Usually someone pushed it.

Step 3

So, we have to accept everything is caused by something else. But hang on, how did the universe start? It had a beginning, it didn't cause itself, so what caused it?

Step 4

Okay, so if there was a beginning to the universe, we have to have something to start it all off. That something had to be uncaused – had to just exist. At some point in the history of the universe there had to be something that wasn't caused by anything else – an Uncaused Cause, Aquinas called it. Can you guess what this Uncaused Cause was?

Step 5

Some people say it was God – Thomas Aquinas said *everyone* believes the Uncaused Cause to be God (but then he was a monk, so we'd expect that!)

The Basics

1 In your own words, explain the idea of God as the First Cause. You could use the domino idea to help you explain.
2 Do you think Aquinas is right to say '*everyone* believes the Uncaused Cause to be God'? Explain your answer.
3 Can you think of anything else that might be the First Cause – other than God?
4 How convincing an argument for God's existence do you think this is? Explain your answer.

Extension Work

Check out Aquinas and try to find out the other 'ways' he used to prove that God exists. They will be helpful to you later in this unit – and so in the exam.

You might say: 'Of course, it's the **Big Bang**! *The Big Bang is the First Cause.' But wait a minute, what caused the Big Bang? Do you think it might have been God? Think about it!*

Now you know the argument from First Cause

The trouble with Thomas

The exam could ask you about the weaknesses in the First Cause argument for the existence of God. So, let's look at this argument more closely.

Can you see any flaws in it? Thomas Aquinas was writing hundreds of years before the internet and modern science. Also, he was a monk, so was more likely to believe what the **Bible** said than any of us.

Use these clues below to work out some of the bigger problems with Aquinas' argument:

a Who does Aquinas say believes the Uncaused Cause to be God? Is this realistic?

b How does he know *everything* is caused by something else? What would be his evidence?

c What is Aquinas' God like? What does the God in this argument do? Does this sound like the Christian God?

Think about clue a. Okay, well, do you really think Aquinas could have asked everybody if they agreed with him? Hundreds of years ago, with no phones or internet? Even if he asked something totally obvious like, 'Do you think water is wet?' he can't really say everybody agreed. He is making a claim that he can't prove.

Clue b is similar. Has Aquinas seen everything? Can he know it is all caused by something else? Can anyone – in their entire life, doing nothing but study – be sure they have seen everything? It is another claim Aquinas can't prove.

What about clue c? Aquinas' God caused the world, full stop, end of! Gods usually carry on, help people and so on, but we don't know about Aquinas' God. Could Aquinas' God have just caused the universe, and then died? Could Aquinas' God have caused a rubbish universe, and not be able to fix it or have deliberately caused evil? This God only has one role. This is a problem because it leaves too many unanswered questions.

The Basics

1 What do we mean by 'problems' in philosophy?
2 What problems are there with Aquinas' First Cause argument?
3 Do you think the problems make his argument weaker? Is it still as convincing as it was to you? Explain your answer.

A word about problems in philosophy

You will see the word 'problem' often in this course. You need to understand what it means in philosophy-speak. It isn't like a health problem, or a problem between people, or a maths problem. It is one of those times where you say, 'Yes, but…' and pose a difficult question for the person who is trying to explain something to you. You will have done it with your parents, or with your teachers, and when they can't answer, we usually feel quite proud of ourselves!

In this course, the *problems* are usually questions that challenge an argument, or challenge **belief**. So you get to ask all those difficult questions about the arguments and watch your teacher and classmates squirm! Seriously though, you have to be able to talk about the problems – the flaws – in all the philosophy we cover, because the exam is going to ask about them.

Now you know some problems with the argument from First Cause

The argument from design (teleological argument)

This is **William Paley**. He said that the world itself was enough evidence of God's existence. It is too amazing to have just happened by chance.

Can you think of something amazing about the world? Why is it amazing?

Paley started by saying if you found a stone, you'd think nothing. But then if you found a watch, you would believe that it had been manufactured – even if you didn't know what it was.

Look at this object. What is it? Has it got a purpose that you can recognise? Is it manufactured or natural? How can you tell?

You probably said that that object wasn't natural. Even if you don't know what it is, it is artificially made. We can tell that things were deliberately made because they obviously have some sort of use and purpose.

Paley said that world is like that watch, or the object you just looked at. There is a difference though – he said the world is even more obviously designed.

There are many patterns in nature – like the food chain and the seasons.

There are so many unique things – like each one of us, our iris pattern, our fingerprints, our DNA.

So many things seem perfectly suited to their environment – like polar bears, which have special fur, and an extra layer of fat to keep them warm.

It must have been God.

Paley said that the world is too amazing for chance. Something, or someone, must have thought about it all and deliberately made it. That someone must have been God.

Person Profile

The most famous person to use the argument from design to prove God's existence was **William Paley**. He was an eighteenth-century archdeacon in Carlisle. He wrote many books, including *Natural Theology*, which contains his 'proof'. His argument followed the process on this page. It is basically saying that the world looks designed, so it must have been – and God was the designer.

4

Now you know the argument from design

Task

Answer these questions before you read on:

1 Outline Paley's design argument for the existence of God.
2 Is this argument convincing to you? Explain your answer.

Doubts about the design argument!

We could argue about whether the world does look designed, but that comes later in the course. Here, we are bothered about what is wrong with the argument itself. So, what do you think? Is this a strong argument? Does it convince you? Is it more convincing than the First Cause argument? You could get asked any of these questions in the exam, so we need to find out some of the glitches in Paley's argument to support your answer to them.

Think about what Paley is comparing at first – a stone and a watch. The stone is discarded because it has no design, but the watch has. Then, Paley compares the watch to the world – the watch is designed, but the world is even more obviously designed. That's great – makes sense – could it be a proof? Small question – is the stone (not designed) part of the world (very designed)? So, shouldn't it also show design? It sounds like Paley changed the rules in the middle of his argument!

Another thing – just because something looks designed, does this guarantee that it really was designed? The discovery of penicillin, which is brilliant as a medicine, was an accident. The material for ladies' tights should have been raincoat material. The guy who made Post-its℗ was trying to invent a glue that bonded two sides for ever and never came unstuck! So, things that look designed might not have been.

And another thing – what is Paley's God like? He just designs the world. Could he have died after doing that? Was it his only design, or are there loads of better or worse designs floating around somewhere? What do you think of God's design? Impressive…or not? I bet there are loads of examples you could give to show the design wasn't as perfect as Paley suggests – have a think. Check out Topic Two to get some ideas if you need to.

The Basics

1 Explain some of the problems with Paley's argument.
2 Check back to pages 2–3. Are any of the problems found in the First Cause argument true for this design argument?
3 Do you think the problems make Paley's argument weaker? Is it still as convincing as it was to you before you explored its problems? Explain your answer.

Extension Work

1 Find out about other design arguments – Newton talked about the design of the thumb being proof enough for him.
2 Find out what 'teleological' means, so you can use it in your exam and impress the examiner!

 Now you know the problems with the argument from design

Miracles – God be praised!

Many people believe that God exists because of miracles. They say God makes miracles happen, and the miracle is the proof that God exists. The miracle is an example of God reaching into our world to help us. Religions are full of stories of miracles. Miracles can confirm what someone already believes – like a proof for their faith. Miracles can also make someone believe in God – the trigger for belief. Without God, there are no miracles.

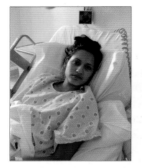

Brought back from death

The name of God in seeds inside the aubergine

Every single person survived

It drank pint after pint of milk

Thousands flock to see image of Mary

Three-year-old child safe after being dragged down a drain

> *These events have all been called miracles. What is a miracle? From these images, how can you explain the idea of a miracle?*

Miracles are usually seen as:

- an act of God – God did it
- going against what we understand of nature – impossible
- helpful or good for people.

Many religious people believe God is **immanent** – interfering in our world through miracles. So, the family whose house is destroyed by a tornado whilst they sleep through it is protected by an act of God.

Miracles are often very **personal**. People think God is showing himself to them by acting in their life for their good. If I have amazing luck, I might believe that luck came from God for me personally. This miracle has proved to me that God exists – and it doesn't matter what anyone else says, I believe in God.

Task

Which word in each pair describes a miracle for you?

- Expected/unexpected.
- Possible/impossible.
- Bad/good.
- Disaster/saving.
- People/God.

You probably picked the second word of each pair – most people would. Can you explain why you picked each one?

The Basics

1 Explain what a miracle is.
2 Give three different examples of a 'miracle'.
3 How does a miracle prove that God exists?
4 If a miracle happened to you – say recovering from a serious illness that could have killed you – would you think it was a miracle? Explain your answer.

Extension Work

Find some different accounts of miracles to use as examples in your work. For each, consider why it has been called a miracle, and what the issues are with giving it that label.

Now you know the argument from miracles

Miracle or coincidence?

You have probably already spotted loads of problems with believing events to be miracles. You might question the reality of a miracle. You might question whether God did it. You might question what it tells us about God.

Let's see if we can work out some of the problems using some examples. (Examples are always really useful for developing your answers in the exam. They gain you more marks.) The questions will help you to discuss and explore the problems.

Situation		Questions
Situation 1 'My dad got dragged into a machine at work whilst trying to fix something. His arm was snapped and paralysed. The doctors said this was permanent. My mum and her fellow churchgoers prayed daily for its healing. My dad doesn't believe in God, so he didn't pray! After eight months, the paralysis was over, and his arm now works fine. Mum says it was a miracle.'		**Questions** 1 What evidence is there for this being a miracle? 2 How do you know the dad didn't think it was a miracle? 3 Why did the mum and dad differ in their ideas?
Situation 2 A school building collapses, crushing a number of pupils to death. Others are seriously hurt, never fully recovering. Others walk away uninjured. The mother of one of those who escaped is heard to say that God has saved her child through a miracle.		**Questions** 1 What was the miracle? 2 Who did it, and why? 3 What do you think the parents of those dead or injured think of God?
Situation 3 At half-time in the Champions League Final, Liverpool are losing 3–0. Liverpool fans all over the world are shell-shocked, praying for something to make the scoreline look reasonable. After full-time, it is 3–3, thanks to Gerrard's God-given talent. Extra time comes and goes. Liverpool win on penalties. This is the 'miracle of Istanbul'.		**Questions** 1 Was this a miracle? 2 Did God answer their prayers? 3 If it was a miracle, what does it tell you about God's use of miracles?

So what did you spot? See if these clues help you:

- Think about what a coincidence is.
- Do people interpret things differently?
- What is God doing for everyone else?

Often 'miracles' are seen as things we can't yet explain, or coincidences. If they aren't performed by God, they do not prove that he exists. Miracles happen to few people, and often to unlikely or undeserving people – which doesn't make God look good. If a person already believes in God, then that might affect the way they interpret an event. All this makes the argument from miracles look shaky – unless it was you it happened to! But there is a problem there …

The Basics

1 Use examples to explain why miracles are a weak way of proving that God exists.
2 Why do you think that people who experience miracles see them as good proof of God?

Now you know some problems with the argument from miracles

Seeing is believing – the argument from religious experience

What would make you believe that God exists? Most of the class probably would say, 'If I met him.' Meeting God is a form of religious experience – an experience of God or the divine.

> God spoke to me in a dream, so God must exist.

Some types of religious experience
Visionary experience

Teresa of Avila claimed to have seen God in visions. Seeing God would prove to anyone that God exists, because you can't see something that doesn't exist (can you?).

Now Teresa is pretty significant because she lived hundreds of years ago and wrote books about her experience. The fact that a woman did that – and went into the history books to be remembered – points to her being special. Few women are remembered in history that far back, and even fewer for their works.

Conversion experience

St Paul met Jesus on the road to Damascus. St Paul converted from being a Jew, who hunted Christians for execution, to being the lead figure in Christian history after Jesus. He met Jesus/God, and the impact on his life was immense.

General revelation experience

Many people feel that God did something for them, or they caught sight of something caused by God, or they got a sense of God's presence. They don't mean they saw him for a chat. They are interpreting their experiences as coming from God, or coming into contact with God. Worship would be a really obvious time to feel God's presence – after all it is for him!

So why does religious experience prove that God exists?

Isn't it obvious? If you meet God, you know he exists (why?). If you go and worship God, you might get a sense of his presence (why?). If you have conversations with God…well, we only talk to real people don't we? The point is, we trust ourselves and our instincts. God forms the other half of a two-sided equation in each case. None of these makes sense without having God as part of them.

You can find out more detail about religious experience – their range – in Topic Two.

The Basics

1 Explain what we mean by 'religious experience'.
2 Explain how religious experiences prove that God exists.

Extension Work

Find out about the 'numinous' – an idea Rudolph Otto had about our experience of God.

Now you know the argument from religious experience

But did you really see what you said you saw?

This is a key problem when we talk about religious experience – can we be sure we really saw what we think we saw? Or did we make it up (consciously or sub-consciously)? Have you ever thought you saw something, only to realise you got it wrong?

Or was it just that you dreamed about God?

What about the person who has the religious experience? Does it matter who they were? Imagine your best friend, who you would trust with your life, came to school tomorrow and told you that they now believe in God because they met him. What would you think? What would you say? Would you believe they met God? Would that make you believe in God? What about if you knew they were quite religious – would that affect your attitude to what they said? Look at the images below – which responses are realistic to you?

What do you think this person means?

Must have been dreaming.

I met God.

This exam stress is getting to him.

Mad.

I'd believe anything he said, so it must be true.

He's such a joker!

I need a new friend.

What about general experiences? They are based on interpretation of things. Look at Situations 1 and 3 on page 7. What do these situations tell you about how different people interpret the things that happen to them, or they see? This is a big problem for the argument because, unless we have the experience, we rely on trusting others. It isn't always easy to do this. People who are generally trustworthy can get it wrong, just as those we never trust do actually tell the truth at times!

Problems with our own experiences

Has anything ever happened to you that no one believed? It can be very hard to convince others of something we know is true. Those meetings with God often have no evidence that we can show to people. Without the evidence, they prove nothing – yet we are trying to use them to prove that God exists. Even if we got God to sign his name, or provide evidence, would people believe? Think about your attitude to miracles – they should be evidence of God, but do you believe in them?

The Basics

1 Why are religious experiences difficult to prove?
2 Why are people often not believed when they say that they met God, or had a religious experience that proves God exists?
3 What conditions would make a religious experience prove that God exists?

It's about what's right and wrong!

Person Profile

Immanuel Kant (1724–1804) was a German philosopher. He was a university professor and wrote many books. He argued that our knowledge came from a source beyond our experience. He also argued that our sense of right and wrong came from something beyond humans themselves. His argument is the most commonly used form of the argument from morality.

Task

Imagine you are creating the rules for a new community of humans who are going to colonise another planet. On your own, write five rules beginning with 'It is right to…' and five rules beginning with 'It is wrong to…'.

Compare your rights and wrongs with a partner or others on your table. How many do you share? Maybe they aren't written in exactly the same way, but the meaning behind them might be the same.

Now compare your rules as a class. Does the class have a core set of rules? Probably there are some that are common to everyone. Certainly you will be sharing values, even if the rules differ. What values can you pick out?

Isn't it amazing how we all have the same ideas, more or less?

The Basics

1 Using examples, explain what we mean by 'morality'.
2 Why is it possible to say that humans have a shared morality? Give some examples to support your answer.
3 What is the 'categorical imperative'?
4 Explain why Kant believed that morality proved God exists.
5 Does this argument persuade you that God exists? Explain your answer.

It is true that if you did that test in the task on any group of people, you'd probably get the same outcome. So where do we all get this shared sense of right and wrong from?

There is a bit more too. Not only do we have this shared sense of right and wrong, we also have a shared sense that we *should* do what is right and *should not* do what is wrong. Usually no one had to tell or force us – we just already knew it. Kant called this the 'categorical imperative'.

Now this sense of having to do something must come from somewhere, and we already saw in the First Cause argument (pages 2–3) that there would have to be an Uncaused Cause of it.

The source of morality and 'we should do…' is the key. With a partner, think of some ideas of what that source might be. Include the strengths and weaknesses of your ideas.

Here are some things to remember about the source:

◆ It can't be human – we live and die. The source would have needed to exist before humans and needs to keep existing.
◆ It has to have intelligence because there is a logic to our morality. We also need to be able to see morality in different situations.
◆ It has to be good because our morality is overwhelmingly good.

So what did you come up with?

Kant certainly believed the answer was God.

Now you know the argument from morality

Morality? What morality?

Wasn't that a brilliant argument for the existence of God? Okay, you know what's coming next! What is wrong with the argument from morality?

Below are some questions for you to think about, and then apply to the argument. Some of them provide you with the problems of the argument, whereas some will help you to understand it better, and perhaps to see it as more persuasive.

1 Does everybody have exactly the same sense of right and wrong?
2 Does everyone share similar values (even though they might go about them in a different way)?
3 Is our sense of right and wrong fixed or changing?
4 Does everybody have the same sense of what we 'should/should not' do?
5 Are there any alternative sources for our morality?

People have argued against this argument from morality in many ways. They question whether we have a sense of shared morality at all. It isn't difficult to find lots of examples where people's ideas of right and wrong are completely different from others. Saddam Hussain ordered Kurdish and Shi'ite villages to be bombed with gas. George Bush – when Governor of Texas – signed the execution permit for more people than any other state governor in American history. Some footballers seem to think it is fine to cheat for a chance of a goal. Some people think hunting animals for fun is good. Some people go diving amongst corals, which are endangered by the very act of diving. We could think of more examples, and argue long and loud about all of them. What does this tell you about your 'shared' morality?

Then again, what about the idea that we should or should not do something? Do people always listen to the voice in their head that says they should? You could argue – well, if there is a voice, it is our free will that makes us ignore it. The Yorkshire Ripper murdered nineteen women because he said a voice (God) told him he should – and there are plenty more examples like that!

Do people everywhere really share the same morality? The head-hunters of Borneo thought that it was right to cut the heads off their victims as a keepsake. Some American Indians scalped their victims. Soldiers in all wars have committed what we consider to be atrocities.

This argument has lots of flaws – but it still rings true for some people. You need to be able to show the examiner that you can argue both sides.

The Basics

1 Explain three flaws in the argument from morality. Use examples to help make your explanation stronger.
2 How effective is the argument from morality in proving the existence of God? Explain *your* opinion.

 Now you know some flaws in the argument from morality

The weight of the arguments

You have just spent a number of lessons learning a series of arguments for the existence of God, and then pulling them to pieces. It might seem as if you can't *prove* that God exists. Well, maybe you can't actually 100 per cent scientifically prove it. That doesn't mean you can't be persuaded by an argument that it is likely or probable that God exists. In this case, you end up *believing* that God exists. This is all to do with the *weight* of the argument you are considering; in other words, how powerful it is.

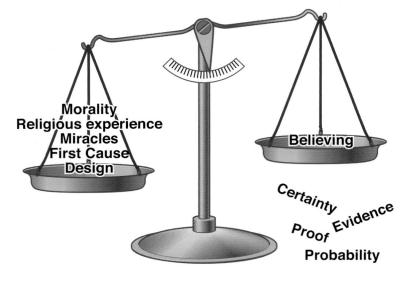

Task

With a partner, discuss which argument you found most persuasive. Explain why.

Then discuss the argument you found least persuasive. Again, explain why.

The task on this page is probably quite difficult, but you have to be able to do it – the exam will expect you to. In fact, you need to be able to do this for any of the arguments – any one could be on the exam.

The easiest way to answer a question about strengths and weaknesses is to state what is good or bad about it in your opinion. If it convinces you or makes you think there might be a God, say so – that is a valid point to make.

Useful words and definitions

Belief an idea accepted as true without positive proof, e.g. belief that God exists.

Proof any evidence that helps to establish a fact, for example, the video footage of John killing Fred, combined with eye-witness and confession statements, was the proof of John's guilt.

Evidence grounds for belief/disbelief, for example, the beauty of the world is evidence it was designed.

Certainty something established as probable, being sure of something, for example, it is certain we will all be sad at some point in our life.

Probability something that is likely to happen or be true, for example, if there is a God, the probability is that he is good.

The Basics

1 What do these words mean: evidence; proof; certainty; probability; belief?
2 Read through each of the arguments for the existence of God. Which word best applies to each argument? Explain your reasons.
3 Which argument do you think is the most convincing? Explain your opinion.

Nope, I still don't believe that God exists!

In spite of all these arguments that try to prove that God exists, many people still don't believe in God. *Why* do you think this is?

Check out this conversation and pick out the reasons being suggested why God doesn't exist.

Gemma: No, I *don't believe there is a God*.

Sol: *Why not?* I *don't either, but those* RE *lessons made me think a bit!*

Gemma: *Well, look, I've never met God. I need to see God to believe in him.*

Sol: *Have you ever seen oxygen?*

Gemma: *Idiot! You can't see it! And don't tell me – you just proved something can be invisible and exist! About those lessons. They were persuasive whilst our teacher was telling us, but after it, well, they didn't work – too full of holes and flaws.*

Sol: *They made me think, so I suppose I could believe in God if I had a bit of proof.*

Gemma: *There is no scientific proof. And I don't believe when somebody tells me they saw God. My gran said she had – but I think she'd had one sherry too many, and she goes to church so thinks that way anyway. You can't rely on her as a witness.*

Sol: *I liked the design argument, but I can think of plenty of bad stuff in the world – and that makes me think there isn't a God, or if there is, he isn't very friendly.*

Gemma: *It's weird, you know, even though my gran believes in God, my dad says it's all made up. He always said there wasn't a God, so I should sort my own problems out. I did try praying one time, but nothing happened. As far as I'm concerned, that proves there is no one to answer them.*

Sol: *I think I'm on your side. But I'm going to be good – just in case!*

People give lots of reasons for not believing in God. Interestingly, a Frenchman called Blaise Pascal said everyone should act as if God existed, just in case he does! The logic is clever – if there is *no God*, when you die, that is it, the end. Nothing to gain or lose. If there *is a God*, and you die as a believer, there are big rewards, heaven and all that. But if you die as a non-believer, there is punishment for not believing. Lots to gain and lots to lose. Pascal said clever people would choose to believe. This is known as 'Pascal's Wager'. What do you think?

The Basics

1 Give four reasons for not believing that God exists.
2 Explain three of your reasons.
3 **You can't see God, so he mustn't exist.** Do you agree? Give reasons for an answer that agrees, and then a reason for one that disagrees.

Now you know some arguments against the existence of God

Agnostic...atheist...theist

Read the speech bubbles below. Who definitely believes in God and who doesn't?

Somebody started the world off...but then again, it might have been an accident, and nobody did it.

Harry

Holy books are the words of God. God spoke to people who wrote them down.

Mich

I have learnt lots of arguments for God's existence – I'm just not sure.

Nath

Nature is too cruel for someone loving to have made it and be in charge of it.

Stevie

Why does God let good people die? Because there is no God, that's why!

Sammi

When God spoke to me in a dream, it made me feel lots better.

Jade

Science explains everything. God is just what we say when we don't know the real answer.

Dawn

I thought about how people behave, and I think our conscience proves there is a God.

Cara

I think the world looks like somebody made it. Some things are too beautiful to be an accident. Some things are too amazing to be a fluke.

Mo

People who believe in God are called **theists**.

But if you don't believe in God, you are called an **atheist**.

And if you aren't sure, you are called an **agnostic**.

a Which are you?
b What makes you say that?
c Which of these words applies to each of the people on the page?
d Can you make up some sentences that each one might say to show what they believe about God?

Research Task

Check out some of the people listed to the right. Find out what their belief is or was and their reasons for their belief. Then find some other names to add to your lists.

Famous agnostics
Matt Groening
Jack Kevorkian
Carl Sagan
Uma Thurman
Charles Darwin

Famous atheists	Famous theists
Lance Armstrong	Isaac Newton
Isaac Asimov	Georges Lemaître
Keanu Reeves	Tony Blair
Fidel Castro	C.S. Lewis
Terry Pratchett	Anthony Flew

Now you know some key words

This topic in the exam

So how will the exam ask about this topic?

Well, there are two kinds of question. The first are knowledge- and understanding-based questions:

1 What is an agnostic?

2 Explain the argument from design for the existence of God.

3 Explain why some people do not believe in God.

This type of question will be worth 9 marks in each full question, divided into two or three sections. You would gain 1 mark for saying what an agnostic was, but the other questions could be worth three or four marks each if they came up.

The other type of question is an evaluative question:

4 **You can't prove God exists.** What do you think? Explain your opinion.

5 **Meeting God is the best way to know God exists.** Do you agree? Give reasons for your answer, showing you have thought about more than one point of view.

The first of these will always be worth 3 marks – get used to practising them, and recognising the format of the question. You can answer from just one point of view for these. The second example will be worth 6 marks, and will always be the last part of the whole question. You have to answer these from two different points of view – give reasons to agree and reasons to disagree. There is always a three-marker and a six-marker in each question. That's 9 marks for evaluation in each full question.

Each full question is worth 18 marks in total.

So how do you get three evaluative marks?

First mark – giving one simple reason for your opinion of the statement.

Second mark – adding another simple reason for your opinion *or* explaining your opinion by writing it in more detail, or using an example to show what you mean.

Third mark – if you just gave two reasons, then explain them both. *Or* explain one of them really fully (two extra bits about the point you made).

Try it

6 **Miracles are just science we don't understand yet.** What do you think? Explain your opinion.

7 **You can't say God doesn't exist, just because you can't see him.** What do you think? Explain your opinion.

8 **The Big Bang, not God, started everything off.** What do you think? Explain your opinion.

 Now you know some exam techniques

Revising this topic

You have probably seen a diagram like this one before in one form or another. They have many names depending on who has created them. We are going to call this one a 'thought map'. They are brilliant to revise from and to, which might sound a bit weird but let's explore it.

Look at the thought map. It has the main topic idea in the centre, and shows how it can be broken down into further topics, which probably made up your different lessons. These then break down further into the pieces of information you learnt in your lessons. The further from the centre, the smaller the detail – always the least easy to remember but where the top marks are in exams. So you could say you need to get to the outer limits in your revision.

This thought map starts at 'Word bank' and goes clockwise – so your brain can remember it more easily.

Thought maps are built outwards from the central topic to the far edge. Some people put all they know about each element of the central topic, one at a time; others add bits randomly. It is your thought map, so you do what suits you.

Add the next layer of this thought map by adding examples, or extra points of information.

So, how does it act as a 'from and to' revision tool? Well, your teacher could give you a complete version, and you could look over it to see how much you are confident about. By highlighting the bits you know well, you end up with some bits that you need to do the serious revision on. You are working 'to' understanding it all.

At the end of the revision period, you can use it as a last-minute checklist – so you'll be revising 'from' it.

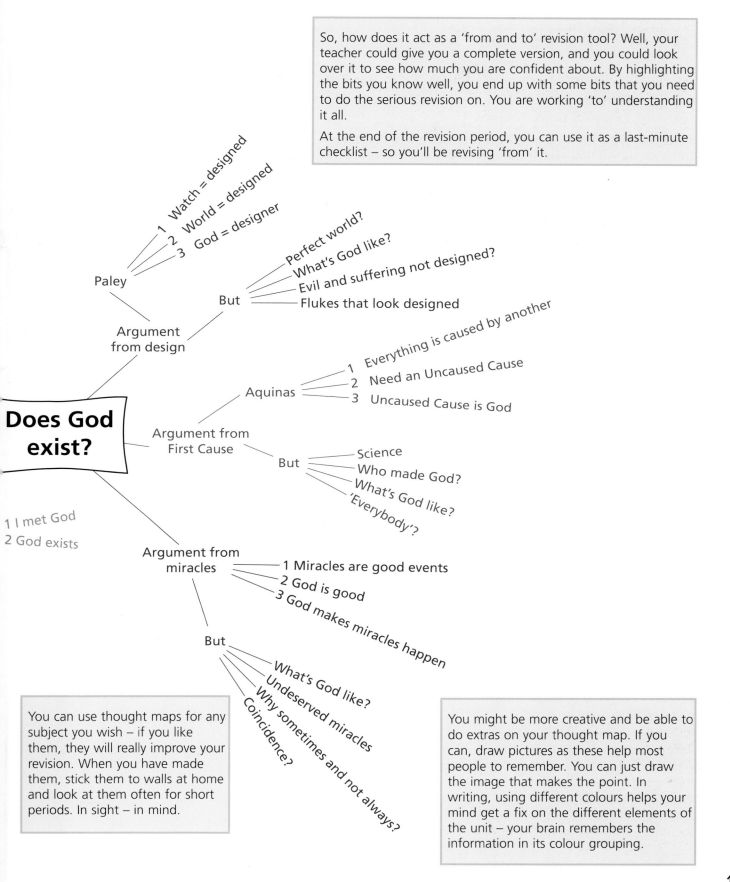

Does God exist?

Paley
1 Watch = designed
2 World = designed
3 God = designer

Argument from design

But
Perfect world?
What's God like?
Evil and suffering not designed?
Flukes that look designed

Aquinas
1 Everything is caused by another
2 Need an Uncaused Cause
3 Uncaused Cause is God

Argument from First Cause

But
Science
Who made God?
What's God like?
'Everybody'?

1 I met God
2 God exists

Argument from miracles
1 Miracles are good events
2 God is good
3 God makes miracles happen

But
What's God like?
Undeserved miracles
Why sometimes and not always?
Coincidence?

You can use thought maps for any subject you wish – if you like them, they will really improve your revision. When you have made them, stick them to walls at home and look at them often for short periods. In sight – in mind.

You might be more creative and be able to do extras on your thought map. If you can, draw pictures as these help most people to remember. You can just draw the image that makes the point. In writing, using different colours helps your mind get a fix on the different elements of the unit – your brain remembers the information in its colour grouping.

Topic Two Revelation

This topic is concerned with *how* people learn about God, particularly through **revelation**. It is linked to Topic One The existence of God because it is one of the 'proofs' of God's existence, since it provides personal evidence for God's existence.

Many people say they will only believe in God when they meet God. Maybe you are one of them. Think about this though – if you met God, could you prove that you had met God? Could you prove it to yourself or anyone else? Would you later dismiss it as an **illusion** or something other than God?

Revelation is when God reveals himself, so that humans can know something about God. There are two kinds of revelation:

---

1 Special revelation
Direct revelation, God communicating directly with you (as an individual or a group). For example, talking to you in a dream, hearing his voice whilst you are praying.

General revelation
Indirect revelation, God revealing something of himself through other things, e.g. nature, people or events. You interpret what you see as being linked with God and this leads you to claim you have experienced God. Your interpretation is based on a feeling.

Learn these two definitions. You may be asked to explain them in the exam.

Let's try to guess some of the questions that could be asked regarding revelation. Then, as we look at some examples of different types of revelation, we can keep these questions in mind. Philosophy is about those questions, and our efforts to find solutions.

Task

Sort the following questions into two categories: those that apply to special revelation; and those that apply to general revelation. Some might apply to both.

Where is the concrete proof that this really happened?

Can you believe someone who already believes in God?

Is there any other explanation?

Are our feelings and interpretations always right?

Does a particular place or context make us see things in a certain way?

Can you answer any of these questions? Have a go.

Now you know what we mean by revelation

Special revelation

Special revelation is a direct revelation – God comes directly to the person involved, and makes himself known. It isn't that we guessed God did something, like cure someone because we prayed for it. It is that God spoke directly to a person. The event can have a massive impact on the life of that person. Unfortunately, there is no scientific evidence of this experience being true that we can show to someone else, or even keep for ourselves. We cannot prove it was real by using science or forensics. How can we show it was real?

Actually, if we can't prove God by scientific means, we won't be able to prove that someone did meet God, will we? All we can do is listen to the person's account of what happened and judge the impact it had on them. Then we have to decide whether or not we believe that they met God – and, from that, whether we now can say God exists.

Let's look at an example from Christianity

1 **Saul** was a Jew who rounded up Christians ready for execution as blasphemers against the Jewish faith.
2 On his way to Damascus, Saul was blinded by a light that only he could see, and from which came Jesus' voice, 'Saul, why do you persecute me?'
3 For three days, Saul was blind. Then a Christian came to cure him, saying God had sent him to do so.
4 Saul immediately became a Christian. He travelled around the Mediterranean spreading the message of Christianity. His teachings form the basis of much of the Christian faith.

For the exam, you may need to be able to describe special revelations from two religious traditions. You will see another example on the next page, which is from Judaism, although it is also part of Christian tradition. When you read the examples, think about the impact they had on the person involved. What difference did it make to their lives?

1 Moses was looking after a flock of sheep that belonged to his father-in-law.

2 A flame suddenly burst from the middle of a bush, yet the bush didn't seem to be getting burnt. Moses decided to go closer to have a look.

3 Suddenly, the voice of God spoke from the bush, telling Moses to take off his shoes because this was holy ground.

4 God then spoke to Moses for a long time, telling him that he had been chosen to help the Israelites to gain freedom from slavery in Egypt.

See Exodus 3 of the Bible for this story.

> If you had been Saul or Moses, what would you have believed had happened? Explain why.

> Do you think that this type of direct experience is the best evidence for God's existence? Explain why.

Extension Work

1 Find out in more detail about either/each of the two examples of direct revelation.

2 Find some other examples of people who have claimed to have met God.

When someone has a special revelation, they feel that they have met God in some direct, clear way. Maybe they have spoken to God, maybe they have heard God, or felt God's presence. Whatever happened, they are convinced this was God, and they know God through this meeting. These experiences can be life changing. In the two examples you have just read, both Saul and Moses completely changed their lives, and put their own lives at risk many times because of their new beliefs.

Can we prove what happened though? To ourselves? To anyone else? This is a problem. But hang on, why would anyone lie about these experiences? Would you tell anyone if they happened to you – if not, why not? It is a big deal to describe these experiences to anyone because of how sceptical we all are.

But then again – TV space, fifteen minutes of fame, money – all good enough to encourage some people to lie, or see things that happen to them in a certain way. So maybe some of these experiences are 'invented'. And again, can we trust people who believe in God – do they expect it to be God, so are biased and unconsciously invent these experiences? There is always the fact that our senses can be deceived by many things – tiredness, illness, drink and drugs…

The Basics

1 Define revelation.

2 What is the difference between special and general revelation?

3 Write accounts of two direct revelations of God and state which religious tradition each comes from.

4 What problems can you find with the idea of direct revelation?

5 **We should always believe it when someone says God spoke to them.** Do you agree? Explain the reasons for your answer.

Now you know some of the debate around special revelation

General revelation: knowing God ...through nature

Nature is beautiful.

Nature is clever.

Nature is complicated.

It seems that there is design and purpose in nature.

These ideas provoke a sense of awe and wonder in many people. This makes people think of God.

Make a list of examples of how nature is each of these things.

Many people would say that the sense of awe and wonder they feel when experiencing nature is a sense of the divine (God) on earth. God is visible through his creation, or in the way that his creation works. This idea can be difficult to get your head around. Let's explain it in a different way. If you like art or music or film or books, you may like a particular person's work. There is something about their style that draws you to them. Even before you hear or see or read their latest work, you might buy it. You can also recognise their work because of the style. When you get used to their style, you may feel it tells you something about them as a person – their thoughts or feelings.

This is very much how some people see the world – it is God's creation and so is full of hints about God. Generally speaking, the world and nature are good – so God is good. The elements of the world, although we try to use the ideas and imitate them, are vastly greater than those we could devise. We could, therefore, say that God is much wiser, cleverer, and more powerful than we are. People are seeing God in aspects of God's creation – God is revealing himself indirectly.

Can you think of any examples of this?

Examiner's Tip

You have already seen these ideas presented elsewhere in this book. We met the idea of nature having been designed in Topic One (pages 4–5). Make sure you can see and use the links between topics, because being able to do so shows a higher level of understanding in the exam. Check it out again to strengthen your ability to answer on this topic.

The Basics

1 How can we know God through nature? Give examples to support the points you make.
2 How well does nature prove that God exists? Explain your answer.
3 Are there any issues with saying God reveals himself through nature? Explain them.

Knowing God...through worship

There are three types of worship – charismatic, sacramental (or ritualistic) and contemplative. Read these accounts given by practitioners of each. Since worship often includes the use of holy books and teachings, there is some overlap into the next topic. However, there is also the feeling of a presence of God, perhaps that God is active in these events, as well. *Does this mean we can know him better?*

Charismatic worship

When I was little, my parents took me to the local church. Then at 18, I visited a Pentecostal church, and was smitten by their services. The people in there were really free with their emotions and love for God. They sang and clapped and danced. To me it looked a little strange, and I must have shown it in my face. Someone took me aside, and explained to me that the people had welcomed the Holy Spirit into their lives. Now they were praising God in a totally uninhibited way. God had accepted them, forgiven them, and was there for them. This sort of stuff is labelled the *gifts of the Spirit*. You just have to open up to God, let him in, and do what he wants you to do. It is really spontaneous. It's also amazing to see people so happy, crying with happiness, people speaking strange languages that you instinctively understand, even people being healed at times. All of this is God working through them. Of course, there is a pattern to our worship, but each person reacts differently. It is as if God uses these people as his voicepiece to the world, and they are seeing him.

Task

How can we define each type of worship from the descriptions given below? Read the following three definitions. Which fits each type?

a This type of worship is quiet, often solitary. It involves focusing on some image or idea. The important elements for the believer are thought, focus and concentration.

b This type of worship is often very happy and lively. People do as they feel moved to do – for some that may mean singing, for others dancing, and so on. It is spontaneous. They let the Spirit of God work through them, granting the gifts of the Spirit.

c This type of worship is very traditional. It follows set patterns, and there is often an element of set wording to it. God's blessing can be received through this type of worship.

Examiner's Tip

Make yourself familiar with how the different types of worship actually look in pictures. You could be asked to identify types of worship, and then say what can be learnt of God from them.

Sacramental worship

I go to church every week. I always take part in the Bread and Wine service, which is at the end of our normal service, once a month. It's always the same; we sit at pews near the altar, and then go to the altar. We each get a piece of bread, which represents Jesus' body, and eat it. Then we are given a small glass of red liquid to represent Jesus' blood. We all drink this at the same time. The minister emphasises that Jesus gave up his life for the sake of our sins, so that we can go to heaven. Although it isn't really Jesus, I certainly feel blessed in some way and refreshed in my relationship with God. Even though it's always the same, I always feel God's love and blessing anew.

Contemplative worship

When I meditate, I always focus on a picture of the Creation. It's quite an old one that I found in a junk shop, but it had something about it. I try to visualise it in my mind, and, as I focus and concentrate, I feel a part of it. I feel closer to God because I am seeing his creation, and appreciating its vastness and wonder. This is a very quiet and still time for me and after it I always feel very refreshed. I also feel that God has guided me through what is a healing time. I suppose it's like prayer in some ways, but I am alone, and it takes much more of my time and focus than I ever gave to prayer. What I still do that I did in prayer is to try and put my problems to God, and listen whilst he helps me to find answers. The quiet and focus is very helpful for this.

The Basics

1 Name each type of worship.
2 Describe what happens in each type of worship.
3 What can people learn about God from worship?
4 Is one type of worship better than the others? In what ways?

Now you know about revelation through worship

Knowing God…through holy books and religious writings

This seems pretty obvious – after all, holy books and religious writings are meant to be about God, aren't they?

Holy books

So what do we learn about God from holy books?

The Qur'an gives 99 names for God. The Bible describes God in many ways.

The Torah gives the Ten Commandments, plus 613 mitzvot (laws). Qur'anic law forms the basis of Shari'ah (Muslim law).

The Old and New Testaments mention God in historical events.

The holy books are all about God, but these three elements stand out: what God is like, how God has acted in the history of the world to influence it, and how God wants us to live our lives.

We can look at holy books in many different ways. Indeed, their believers make different claims for them. The way we view a holy book will decide how closely we follow it, how we treat it, and how we understand what it tells us about God. If I take a book literally, for example, I believe every word to be accurate, so my God will be exactly as described – and I will have to follow the rules exactly.

Religious writings

How are these different from holy books? Well, they are the writings of religious people to explain what is written in the holy books, or their own experiences of God, or the teachings of their religious tradition.

Perhaps the most famous religious leader in the world is the Pope. Head of the Catholic Church, he has written papers about Church teaching. He is also said to be speaking the **infallible** word of God when speaking *ex cathedra*. Roman Catholics look to the teachings of the Pope for guidance in their religious lives.

> *Do we really need people to do this for us?*

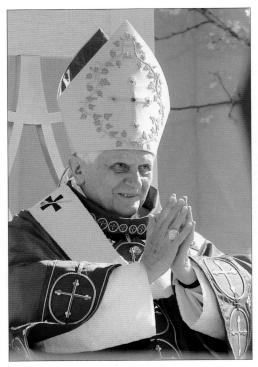
Pope Benedict XVI

Currently enjoying a high profile is the Dalai Lama, the leader of the Tibetan Buddhist faith. The Dalai Lama has become more famous as Buddhism has spread in the West, and because of the Free Tibet campaigns. He has written a series of books that try to put ancient Buddhist teachings into modern language, to make them accessible and readable for the West. In fact, one of these publications, *Ancient Wisdom, Modern World*, was top of the bestseller list for many weeks in 2001.

The Basics

1 What are holy books and religious teachings? Give examples of each.
2 What can we learn of God from these? Give examples.
3 How useful is either in helping us to know about God? And, how well can we know God through these?

Now you know about revelation through holy books

Knowing God...through conscience and behaviour

Some people think God speaks to them through their conscience. Your conscience is the voice in your head, which makes you feel bad when you misbehave, or encourages you to do the right thing. Some believe God tells them to behave in a certain way, and to do certain things. God is acting as their guide.

If a person acts out God's wishes, are we seeing something of God? We interpret what we are seeing, we aren't seeing God directly. They had a revelation, and become a revelation themselves.

Here is an example:

Fred Smith believes he should help those in need because God has told him to through the voice that is his conscience. He works helping the down-and-outs in Manchester. Now, we could say that we can see God through Fred. Fred is doing what he believes God wants him to do: help others. He believes that God has told him to do this – it is a kind of duty for him.

There are many people who have devoted their lives to helping others. That they claim to be led by God suggests God is loving and caring. There are many people who seem close to God. Some people do lots of truly good things. They set examples, and we learn from them. Many of them claim that God has spoken to them directly. We see God through their actions and words indirectly.

The Basics

1 What is 'conscience'? How could this be a revelation?
2 Is this strong evidence of God's existence? Explain your answer.
3 **God talks to each of us through our conscience.** What do you think? Explain your opinion.

Martin Luther King Jr. fought for and gained equal rights for black Americans. He was a Baptist minister, and believed God was using him to change America. His God was a God of love and peace, who called all men equal. Martin fought in a non-violent (peaceful) way. Find out about his work.

Mother Teresa believed that God had called her to help the poor and dying in Calcutta. She also claimed that God guided her to do all the good things she did through her conscience. She set up orphanages, hospices, clinics, schools and leprosy units for the poorest and least-cared-for of Indian society. Following Jesus' teaching about the Final Judgement in Matthew 25:34–40, she believed that when you help the hungry, lonely, sick or poor you do it for God. Mother Teresa said God spoke to her, and she herself became an indirect revelation of God.

So, what does revelation tell us about God?

Every time we meet a person, whether for the first time or the hundredth, we can learn something about them, or get to know them a little better. Over time, our whole attitude to what they are like can change radically – we see them in new situations, and get to see how they operate. So, it figures that every time someone meets God, they learn something about God. The holy books are an example of passing that knowledge on, as is worship.

So, what do we learn?

Have a think – what do the following tell us about God?

> The ecosystem, which is intricate and complicated and keeps everything alive and in balance.

> A holy book, which tells how God looked after and guided his people in difficult times.

> A service in a place of worship, which is focused around praising God through hymns and prayer.

> The work of Mother Teresa.

> A miraculous cure or event.

You might have said these tell us that God is: wise/intelligent, good, the creator of everything, the one who keeps things going. So, as you can see, we have learnt about God through these events.

Key words for God

There are several key words that will impress the examiner if you use them, and which you might get asked about:

Supremacy means God is the best and most in everything – the absolute top!

Immanence means God is involved in the world he created. Coming to earth as Jesus, performing miracles, visiting people – they are examples of immanence.

Transcendence means God is beyond space and time, and totally different to us. He isn't a part of the world, but is beyond it and doesn't get involved.

Personal means you can build a close relationship with God, like having a good friend.

Impersonal means you can't get close to God. God is too powerful really for that – it wouldn't be proper!

Omnipotence refers to God's complete powerfulness, beyond anything we can know. One of the reasons God can do anything.

Omniscience refers to God's total intelligence, again beyond anything we can know or copy. One of the reasons why God could create the world.

Benevolence refers to God's unquestioning and absolute love for his creation. This leads to him helping and caring for us.

The Basics

1 Write out each of the key words for God, and add an explanation alongside in your own words.
2 Write a sentence using each of the key words to show you understand what it means.
3 For each type of revelation, state which characteristics of God are revealed to us.
4 **God can't be both transcendent and immanent – that is impossible!** Do you agree? Give reasons for your answer, showing that you have thought about more than one point of view.

Now you know about the nature of God revealed

Reality or illusion?

Hang on though, that is all great, but…is it all real? If we don't know God exists, how can we know this is all God's work? I know loads of people who don't believe there is a God – they'd all say this was someone putting a spin on things, and getting it wrong!

This is a valid point. Is it **reality** or just an illusion?

The big question is whether people have really met God, or have just imagined it. Reality is what has really happened – you existing is a reality. Illusion is a false or misleading perception – you think you saw a leprechaun in your garden.

Some people say religious experiences are real. Some people say religious experiences are illusions. Some say they can be either – and it all depends on the person and the circumstances.

I just met God.

Yes, dear. I know.

If someone doesn't believe in God, they will think all religious experiences are illusions. You can't meet something that does not exist! These people say there is no proof of God. They also say there is no proof of the experience – it's just what someone says. The person who had the experience could be mistaken, ill, or deliberately lying. They could make themselves believe something that wasn't real because they are so desperate to see God. They might interpret something as being God that isn't really, for instance, if someone was very ill but got better. They may see that as God, but the atheist wouldn't. There is no proof of either, in spite of how strongly convinced they each may be. That is the big problem with religious experiences – they can't be proved, they can only be persuasive.

The person who has the experience might be convinced that it was God, even if they can't prove it. We trust our own instincts and feelings. We can't prove them to anyone else. We might be able to persuade someone else that we met God because of what we say. To the person meeting God, their experience is real – others might see it as an illusion.

YEAH, I HEAR YOU!

The Basics

1 Explain what we mean by 'real' and 'illusion'.
2 What explanations could someone give for a 'religious experience' other than God?
3 **God is an illusion.** Do you agree? Explain your opinion.

Now you know about the reality/illusion debate

Bringing things together

You have seen a whole range of examples of special and general revelation. These all tell us some things about God and that we can know God. You do need to be able to think across the topic though – not just that we can know, or what we can know, but also the reliability of what we can know. These questions come up in Topic One – is it proof of God to have met God? Can you prove God exists at all?

> *Are we really seeing God or are we deluding ourselves? Can we explain religious experiences in any way other than through God? If God is transcendent, can we expect to meet him? If we can meet God, does that mean he can't be impersonal?*

This page is designed to get you thinking about these questions. Look upon it as a sort of brain aerobics session!

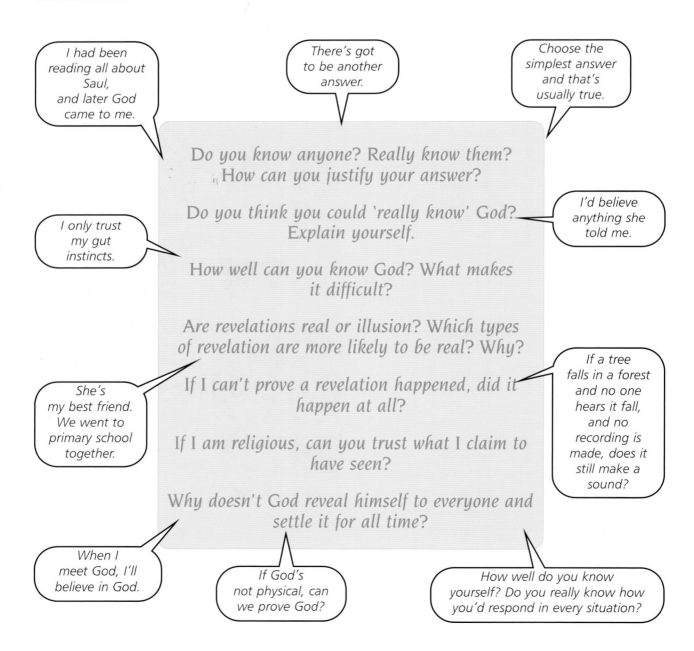

I had been reading all about Saul, and later God came to me.

There's got to be another answer.

Choose the simplest answer and that's usually true.

Do you know anyone? Really know them? How can you justify your answer?

Do you think you could 'really know' God? Explain yourself.

I'd believe anything she told me.

I only trust my gut instincts.

How well can you know God? What makes it difficult?

Are revelations real or illusion? Which types of revelation are more likely to be real? Why?

If I can't prove a revelation happened, did it happen at all?

If a tree falls in a forest and no one hears it fall, and no recording is made, does it still make a sound?

She's my best friend. We went to primary school together.

If I am religious, can you trust what I claim to have seen?

Why doesn't God reveal himself to everyone and settle it for all time?

When I meet God, I'll believe in God.

If God's not physical, can we prove God?

How well do you know yourself? Do you really know how you'd respond in every situation?

This topic in the exam

Glossary building

Did you ever have to learn lists of words? Perhaps you did for languages, or at primary school. You need to do it for your GCSEs as well – sorry! You could be asked what any of the words mean in questions like these:

1 Give an example of general revelation.

2 State two types of religious experience people may have.

3 What is the difference between general and special revelation?

You need to understand the words for all questions in all topics. Say a question worth 4 marks is about special revelation, and you don't know what it is – you have thrown away 4 marks. Start a glossary (word list) and write the technical language in it as you meet it. Add pictures to help you remember.

Levels of response questions

Let's take this opportunity to look at levels of response style questions for attainment target AO1. These are questions about knowledge and its application. The higher the level, the higher the mark awarded. Levels of response reward the depth and breadth of your answer, as well as its coherence. Let's look at how levels of response questions worth 3 marks work:

Level	Description	Mark
1	A simple answer, makes just one relevant point. This is where you write the first thing you think of, and then move on. It isn't explained, or justified.	1
2	If you gave a short explanation of that first thought, or gave an example of it, having stated it, you'd have pushed your mark into Level two (depth). At times, if you've just given several simple reasons you get Level two (breadth).	2
3	This needs more than one reason and explanations, because it is about breadth and depth. Alternatively, you could give just one reason, which you have very clearly and fully explained.	3

Try to answer the following questions, writing a response for each level to see how one level builds on the previous one.

1 Explain why some people say that all forms of revelation are illusions and not real. *(3 marks)*

2 How might a religious believer respond to the claim that God does not seem to be making himself known today? *(3 marks)*

Topic Three The problems of evil and suffering

What do the words 'evil' and 'suffering' mean to you? What is the difference? For the exam, you need to know the words, their meaning and some examples. They cause problems for people who believe in a loving God – so you need to know the sorts of problems they cause. People have tried to explain why God allows these things to happen – we call these explanations **theodicies** – defences of God. You need to know about these. You also need to be able to discuss how people respond to evil and suffering – both their own and that around them.

Have a look at these events:

FOOT AND MOUTH OUTBREAK MEANS THOUSANDS OF ANIMALS SLAUGHTERED

FLASH-FIRES IN RECORD NUMBERS IN GREECE

EARTHQUAKE FLATTENS CITY

MORE REFUGEES FLEE ELECTION AGGRESSION IN ZIMBABWE

OLD MAN MUGGED AND LEFT FOR DEAD

FLOODED – THREE WEEKS AFTER PREVIOUS FLOOD DAMAGE REPAIRED

CAT LOSES EYE IN AIR RIFLE ATTACK

PIRATES ATTACK SAIL BOAT – TWO DEAD

BUG EPIDEMIC WIPES OUT HARVEST

TORTURED – FOR £3.56

Did you notice that some events can be blamed on people? Some are no one's responsibility. Some make us feel angry. Some are simply unfair. Some are downright cruel, or even evil.

We can split them up into two major groups.

The first group are all natural events, they are part of nature. They result in pain for living beings, even death. Often it is simply a case of being in the wrong place at the wrong time – like a hurricane hitting the place you go on holiday. We call this **natural evil**.

The second group are caused by humans – deliberate acts of unkindness, even evil, which cause pain to other beings. Often the actions were thought out, and intended to cause harm. We call this **moral evil**, or evil.

Suffering is the pain caused by these kinds of evil.

Can you separate the headlines above into groups? What sorts of things are you seeing?

Extension Work

Carry out an internet search for 'evil' and 'suffering' – see how many hits you get. Get a few examples of each – following the descriptions above – so that you can give a range of examples in your arguments later in the topic.

Now you know the definitions of evil and suffering

We've got problems!

> So, God is omnipotent, which means he can do anything at all. That's how he created the world.

> He is also benevolent – he loves us all. Loves each one of us, and wants us to be safe and happy. Like a perfect parent.

> And God is **omniscient** – he knows everything it is possible to know. That's like God knowing everything that everybody who has ever lived knows, and then knowing even more. Must have been really clever to design and make the world.

> How come the world has got so much pain and trouble in it? It seems to me that God has a lot of explaining to do. He's powerful enough to stop it all; he knows about it all, and how to stop it; and he loves us enough to want to do something about it. So why doesn't he?

The person questioning God has looked at the big picture and seen the problems. There is one huge problem to do with evil and suffering, and that is: Why does a God who is **all-loving**, **all-powerful** and **all-knowing** allow such pain and misery? The exam wants you to be able to see that problem and try to explain it, but also to break it up into a number of smaller problems.

Look at the newspaper headlines again. Imagine there is a God who created the world, who is all-loving, all-powerful and all-knowing. What sorts of questions could you ask that God because of these incidents? What do these incidents suggest about God's love, power, intelligence, and even God's creation?

You might also think about how *fair* the sharing out of evil and suffering is – what does that tell us about God? What do all these things tell us about how much God looks after his creation?

There are lots of small questions to ask – they all challenge belief in an all-loving, all-powerful and all-knowing God. If they make you think that God isn't as powerful, for example, then it isn't God! So they actually challenge belief in God itself! This is why this topic is such a big deal for religious believers. It makes atheists stay as atheists, and turns theists into atheists, or at least agnostics. It makes some people say that it makes no sense to believe in a God at all in our world.

Religious people have tried to explain the problems of evil and suffering. We are going to look at some of their attempts. You have to remember that, at the end of it all, religious belief is just belief. Belief is usually in spite of anything else, and many religious people don't have a problem with evil and suffering because their belief is stronger than the doubts raised.

The Basics

1 What is the major problem linked to the existence of evil and suffering?
2 What specific problems are caused regarding:
   a. God's love
   b. God's power?
3 Why do some people claim God is unjust?
4 **Evil and suffering prove God doesn't exist.** Do you agree? Explain your opinion.

 Now you know the problems of evil and suffering

About moral evil

> *Where did all this evil begin?*
> *How did it ever come about? Can we blame God?*

These are questions you might need to answer in the exam, so let's consider them.

The Fall

If you read Genesis 3, you will find the story of how Adam and Eve ate the fruit of the Tree of Knowledge. This made them see the difference between good and evil. They were thrown out of Eden (**paradise**), and then made to take responsibility for themselves. The fact that they could now see the difference between good and evil – they could choose – meant that evil existed as a reality. So free will causes evil. God made evil possible by giving free will, but humans have actually created real evil.

Satan

> *So who is to blame – God or man?*

In the Bible, the first time we hear of the **devil** is in the Gospels (Matthew, Mark, Luke and John). They describe the devil trying to tempt Jesus. The devil is named Satan (which is the Hebrew word for adversary). Thomas Aquinas, in the eleventh century, suggested that this figure was actually a fallen angel. He claimed that one of the highest angels had become proud and challenged God. God threw him out of heaven, and he has opposed God on earth ever since.

All in the mind

> *Could this be the solution to the problem of evil? An evil being?*

Many people say evil is within us all as a hidden force. We don't all show it in the same way. If we are brought up in some terrible way, or have friends who influence us to be like this, or have some terrible experience in our lives, then the evil within us can be triggered. So it isn't a force that overtakes us, it's something within – a psychological phenomena.

An impersonal force

> *Can you think of examples to demonstrate this?*

Some people don't think evil is controlled or organised. They see it as a part of nature. It is a negative force, which generates pain on a totally random basis. Not everyone who has a terrible upbringing or experience behaves in an evil way. If it is a random force in nature, then that may explain why not everyone reacts in the same way to their upbringing.

> *Does this explain evil for you?*

The Basics

1 What is evil? How did it originate?
2 How are people themselves responsible for evil?
3 **Evil is within a person and is not a power outside human beings.** Do you agree? Explain your opinion.

32   Now you know the origins of moral evil

The problem with moral evil

Well, essentially it all comes back to God. No one has ever been able to explain in a good enough way *why* there is evil. But hang, on – we just did, didn't we?

Let's have a look at those theories, and see if there are any problems. There is a friend to help...

> With a partner, have a look at each of the ideas, and try to find faults in them.

The Fall

Great story! It makes sense too – until they use their free will (and get into trouble for it), everything is perfect. But you have to ask why God made that tree in the first place. Did he really need to? You could also ask why he told them not to eat from it – guaranteed to make someone do the opposite! God is supposed to be really, seriously clever – so he should have known what would have happened. Sounds like he could have set them up to me – and that is NOT FAIR! And what about everyone still getting affected by evil – they had nothing to do with that apple!

Satan

Come on – a mega-powerful being who can oppose God! Don't believe it! God is meant to be the most powerful being of all. If God wanted to, he could just dispose of the devil for once and for all. *Because nothing is meant to be more powerful than God.* So my question to you is – why is God allowing the devil firstly to continue to exist, and secondly to hurt the creation God is meant to love all the time?

All in the mind

Yes, I can see the logic of this. Most of my friends can be a little bit evil sometimes! However, where did it all come from in the first place? God created everything, we are told, so God must have created the gene or whatever it is that makes us evil. Like I said earlier – so clever, so he must have known what would happen if he created this tiny gene-thing. Problem there! And another thing, why do some very evil people exist who have never had a scrap of nastiness in their own lives? Come from loving homes, turn into murderers...explain that!

An impersonal force

Same as before – God made everything. Makes God look a bit less than perfect, whether he created this either by accident or deliberately. If God did it deliberately, what is the point – it just hurts his creation that he is supposed to love? If he did it accidentally, he isn't as good as he is made out to be.

The Basics

1. For each of the four explanations for evil, give two reasons why it is not a complete explanation.
2. Which explanation do you think is the strongest? Explain why.
3. **God, not the devil, is responsible for evil.** Do you agree? Give reasons and explain your answer, showing you have thought about more than one point of view.

✓ Now you know the problems with the explanations for moral evil

About natural evil

We can argue that evil isn't really about God. Let's ignore the 'random force in nature' idea, and say it is a consequence of our free will – our ability to make decisions, good and bad. The devil works on us through our free will. We choose to behave the way we do because we can. Without free will, we are just puppets really – so free will gives us freedom. If God was to fix our free will, so we always chose a certain pattern of behaviour, or if God hadn't given us free will, then we wouldn't be independent beings. So, even though God must have known what might happen (really clever, remember), he had to go through with it anyway. When we misuse our free will, we have to take the consequences. So God can't be to blame.

What about natural evil though? That is the things that happen in nature, but which cause hurt and pain to living beings – suffering. God made everything, so that must be down to God. So the question becomes:

Why does God allow suffering to exist?

Devastating tsunami

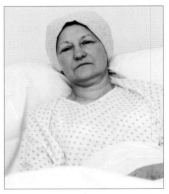

Cancer patient dying in hospital

Earthquake victims

Conjoined twins

> ## Task
>
> Look at these examples of natural evil – what possible reasons could God have for allowing them to happen, and allowing all the suffering they cause? What good could come out of any of them (and who for)?

> *Why do your parents let you suffer, or even make you suffer sometimes?*

There have been many attempts to answer the big question of why God allows suffering. Remember that we call them *theodicies* – defences of God. It helps if we think of God as a parent, which is actually how many Christians see God, and is what Jesus meant when he used the word 'Abba' about God. Your parents sometimes let you suffer for what they see as a good reason.

Theodicies – defending God

Defending God 1

All pain is a punishment for the things we do, say or think that are wrong.

Everybody does things wrong, and not everybody seems to get what they deserve for those things. So, the pain we feel through acts of evil and suffering is simply a punishment for our own badness. God is punishing us.

Can you think of any examples that might back up this defence?

Defending God 2

Pain is a test of our faith in God.

The pain and suffering we feel is a test. In the Old Testament, there is the example of Job. Job's family is killed, his wealth lost, his animals and servants killed or stolen, his property is destroyed and his health taken away. Even his wife is fed up with him! This all happens in spite of the fact that Job is a good man, who worships God. These terrible events, which happened in quick succession, were a test of his faith. He passed the test and became rich again. If we view our own misfortune and pain as a test, and we get through it, we will be rewarded by God.

Can you think of any examples that might back up this defence?

Defending God 3

All pain is part of an education for our souls. We learn from it.

Pain and suffering teach us the difference between right and wrong, between appropriate and inappropriate behaviour, and make us stronger. They teach us greater responsibility for ourselves, for others and for the world around us. We are learning to take care of what God has given us by reacting positively in negative situations. Bad things happen when we don't take responsibility.

Can you think of any examples that might back up this defence?

Defending God 4

There has to be badness for us to understand and appreciate goodness.

This means that we have the bad so that we recognise the good. There has to be a balance for either to exist. So just accept it as part of the *rich tapestry of life.*

Can you think of any examples that might back up this defence?

Defending God 5

Evil and suffering are a result of free will.

Can you think of any examples that might back up this defence?

Obviously, evil is caused by people making the wrong decisions. We were given free will by God. When it is our own choice, we can't blame God, can we?

What about suffering? Is that to do with our free will? It has been suggested that every action, thought and word has a positive or negative effect. These can be felt by us directly, or experienced indirectly, when they affect others. What if they create a force? The negative force will cause natural evil to happen somewhere. If we change our behaviour, we can make a difference.

Defending God 6

Don't question God. Accept God's will.

Can you think of any examples that might back up this defence?

We are only human, and God is rather more special than we are. In fact, God is better in every way. God is transcendent – that is to say, God is beyond our understanding. We can't hope to understand God, so how can we understand what goes on in God's world? We can't see the big picture. So we should not bother trying to work out an answer to the problem – we were wrong even to pose it in the first place.

Defending God 7

It isn't God who causes the evil and suffering. It's the devil.

Can you think of any examples that might back up this defence?

When something bad happens, it's the devil causing it because he is bad. So the devil makes the flood happen out of sheer nastiness. Anything a person does, which is evil, is also caused by the devil because he is controlling them.

The Basics

1 Why do Christians need to defend God?
2 In what ways do Christians defend God? For each defence, give an example to make your point clearer.
3 Do you think the solutions given here are adequate? Do they solve the problem of evil and suffering? Explain, giving reasons and examples.

Research Task

Find out what St Augustine, Leibnitz or Spinoza said about evil – what it is, how it came about, and why it is allowed to continue.

Now you know the solutions to the problem of natural evil

Problems with solutions

You know by now that we have to do this. We have to work out whether the solutions philosophers have given us are strong or weak – and why. You have to make a personal estimation of how good they are because you might get asked for this in the exam.

As you were reading and thinking about those solutions to the problem of natural evil, did you come up with any problems with the solutions?

It is always easier to come up with problems if you have some examples to use. You will often use examples in an argument about something – it is the thing that proves your point or contradicts/messes up someone else's. Below are some examples of suffering. For each, think whether the solution is good enough to explain the suffering (explain it yourself), and decide if the example spoils the solution – at least in those cases. Don't forget – God is supposed to be all-loving, all-powerful and all-knowing, the creator of all. By the way, all the examples are real!

The 'nicest, kindest man in Manchester' dies of cancer. He has just retired, having worked all his life and saved for his retirement, which he intends to enjoy with his wife. His suffering in the last few months was extreme and constant.	Floods in Myanmar caused by a cyclone cause the deaths of over 100,000. Another million are without homes, food, medical care or sanitation due to the destruction caused by the cyclone.	Drought continues in parts of Africa. The harvest is ruined; people and animals starve to death. Aid begins to come from across the world, but it is too late for tens of thousands of people – particularly the old, young and women who are pregnant.	A baby is born with deformities and brain damage. It's so severe, that she is in constant pain for the few days that she lives. Family are devastated because they can do nothing but watch her suffer, and pray for a speedy end.

Extension Work

Collect some newspaper/internet examples of natural evil. How do the solutions apply to each of the examples you find? Do they explain them adequately or not? Why?

The Basics

1   Do you think the solutions given solve the problem of evil and suffering in these cases? Explain your opinion.
2   **We will never solve the problem of evil and suffering.** Do you agree? Give reasons for your answer, showing you have thought about more than one point of view.

Now you know the problems with the solutions to natural evil

Responding to evil

There seems to be so much evil and suffering in the world. It certainly causes many people to believe there is either no God, or no good God. To many, it proves that God does not exist – backing up their atheist belief. However, religious people are like everyone else – they see and experience evil and suffering just as everyone else does. Yet, there are millions of believers who suffer and don't lose faith. It is also the case that when people face evil and suffering, it can actually give them a reason to believe in God. The exam will want to know about how people respond.

There are two ways of responding – responding to personal experience, and responding to other's experience. When we say 'responding', we mean 'what the evil and suffering makes you do'. We are only interested in the good things, or the positive side of it for this exam.

Responding to personal experience

When bad things happen, I try to find the good in them. There is always something, you know, every cloud has a silver lining.

Sherelle

God always knows best. When bad things happen, I accept them and get on with it.

Adam

I see my troubles as a test from God. If I keep believing, I pass. The experience makes me stronger.

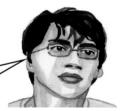

Raj

I know that I have many friends in the church who I can turn to for support. They are God's helpers, and the fact God works in the world like that gives me great comfort.

Cara

God helps me at bad times. He won't let me suffer too much, and he will take away my pain. If the pain was too bad, God would take me to be with him, so I can still have hope even in very bad times.

Theo

I pray and get strength from that. God is hearing my prayer, and is with me.

Zak

My child died. I feel comforted because I know she is with God in heaven.

Jess

Extension Work

Look up the 'Footprints' poem. It is a good way to explain the points made on this page.

Responding to the suffering of others

It would be helpful to think these questions through because they give us some of the motivation for people helping others, as well as show how evil and suffering can lead to good.

Read the following accounts. For each, what is the suffering? Is it because of natural or moral evil? How is the person responding?

> *Just what is it that makes us help people? Is it what everyone does? Is it that some people are kinder than others? Or are some situations more needy than others?*

1 I saw the events of Chernobyl – a nuclear power station disaster. I felt I should try to help the children who live near Chernobyl, so I fund-raise and send money to the orphanages in that area.

2 I was a doctor in the UK, but went to work for Médecins Sans Frontièrs in the Sudan. We help the refugees who are fleeing conflict and starving.

3 I work for Oxfam to raise money for developing countries. I know of famines in several countries, and my work helps to ease those problems a little.

4 I give up a few hours each week as a volunteer in my local hospice, talking to the dying.

5 A child went missing from my town last week. I helped with the searches. The parents were distraught.

6 I visited Vietnam where I had fought in the war. I gave my medals to a museum there – my way of saying sorry for my involvement in the war. I am going to work for a few months as a volunteer in one of their clinics that treats the victims of landmines who had limbs blown off.

For each of these accounts, the person's response to suffering is a positive one. They may or may not believe in God, they simply feel they should do something to make things better – even if they can't make it much better.

You may have seen adverts on TV that show suffering – of people and animals – and which made you want to help. Human nature is to help, to respond positively to other people's suffering. For religious people, they might see helping as a duty from God, or a responsibility of everyone. They might think that helping others is a way to help themselves, for example, to gain entry into heaven, or to develop as a person.

Research Task

Find out about some of the volunteer organisations that exist. Why do people join them and work for them?

The Basics

1 How do people respond positively to their own suffering? Give examples.
2 How does religious belief help people who are suffering? Give examples.
3 How do people respond positively to other people's suffering? Give examples.
4 Why do you think religious belief makes people want to help others?
5 **Evil and suffering bring goodness into the world.** Do you agree? Give reasons for your answer, showing you have thought about more than one point of view.

Now you know about responses to suffering

This topic in the exam

Well, you are going to be asked questions in the following areas: definitions; problems caused for believers; solutions to problems; problems with problems; and, how people respond positively to suffering. You will also have to evaluate statements about any of these. You have seen lots of examples of these already in the topic.

This exam has 6 mark evaluation questions, so let's look at one of these.

It is impossible to defend God when it comes to evil and suffering. Do you agree? Give reasons for your answer, showing you have thought about more than one point of view.

To get full marks there are certain things you have to have done, so let's see how the marks progress. This is called levels of response marking – after the first 2 marks, it is about the depth and breadth of your answer.

Level	Description	Mark
1	A simple comment that shows WHY you agree or disagree with the statement.	1
2	Some simple comments that show WHY you agree and/or disagree with the statement.	2
3	A series (e.g. four or more) of simple comments that show WHY you agree and disagree with the statement. *Or* a couple of statements that are explained, and which show WHY you agree/disagree.	3

Let's take a break there because it is really easy to get to 3 marks – as you can see. Remember, if you get 3 out of every 6 marks, you should get a C grade!

To get more marks, we really have to step up our game. You are going to have to make sure of three things – you include some religious element in your answer (after all it is an RE exam!) You also need to both agree AND disagree – you might just get 4 marks for a really good one-sided answer, but not many people can write those, so take the safe choice and do two sides. You also need to make sure you have given good explanations on both sides of the argument, so that it is balanced. So let's look at those higher levels (and marks).

Level	Description	Mark
4	Two sided with religious content. This answer gives a few comments on each side and explains some of them on each side. *Or* one side of the argument is really well explained, with a simple idea of the other side.	4
5	Two sided with religious content. This answer gives good explanation of both sides through several, reasoned explanations of each side.	5
6	Two sided with religious content. This answer gives very good explanation of each side, using lots of reasons for each side which are developed by explanation and perhaps example. The whole answer flows as you read it, and is a very clear debate.	6

Gosh! Level 6 sounds quite tough! Not to worry, 5 out of every 6 marks will get you an A*, and once you get your teeth into a question, it can flow well anyway.

So, what do they look like?

Read these answers to the exam question on the previous page, then see if you can work out what mark they would have been awarded.

Answer 1

I agree with this. There is too much horrible stuff to say God just doesn't know or something like that. He should be stopping it all – well, bad stuff good people suffer, at least.

Answer 2

On one hand I agree. Why is he letting it happen? I mean, he must be, because of the fact he is supposed to be ultra clever, and ultra powerful, and ultra good. He must know about it, and be letting it happen, if he didn't make it in the first place. If he was as powerful as Christians say – he'd stop it, and as clever as they say – he'd know it was happening, so he'd use his power to stop it, and as loving as they say – he'd want to stop it. It goes on and on – floods, murders, earthquakes, wars. So I reckon you can't defend God at all – not the one Christians talk about anyway.

Answer 3

No, because I don't think there is a God, so he can't be blamed. If there is a God, he might be letting it happen for a good reason, like as a punishment, like for people who rob banks then get cancer. Maybe, God knows stuff we don't, so he has got a reason, but we don't get it. But if you think about it, you could agree too. God lets too much evil and suffering happen, and especially to good people and people who can't be blamed for doing things wrong, like babies. To me, that means you can't defend God, like the statement said. Letting people suffer as a punishment is too bad for some people and what they have done wrong. I suppose it could be the devil – making all the evil happen by influencing people and the weather. Then you can't blame God for the evil and suffering (just for letting the devil get away with it!)

You can use the levels table to practise doing these kinds of questions. You will have to answer four on this exam paper, and if you are doing a full GCSE, four on the other paper too. Good technique is really crucial in the exam – and you learn that by practising.

Try another, using the levels to guide you:

All suffering is a punishment from God. Do you agree? Give reasons for your answer, showing you have thought about more than one point of view. (6 marks)

Commentary

Answer 1

The idea of 'too much' and 'bad stuff good people suffer' are two simple ideas. Neither is expressed very clearly, but both are valid points to make and just about enough to get 2 marks. To get 3 marks, it needs a few more ideas and a bit of explanation would help too.

Answer 2

There are several ideas in this one that link together to make one strong argument, and most of them have a bit of development to show deeper thinking about the points made. Unfortunately, only one side is given (in spite of the opening sentence). This is worth 3 marks. One simple statement on the other side would have gained it 4 marks.

Answer 3

Two sides – good. Two ideas on each side, with a bit of development – better. Examples are used as well – even better. This answer is worth 5 marks. To get 6 marks, it really only needs to be a bit more balanced – say another idea to start with.

Revision tip 1 – Breadcrumbs

When you work on the internet, you might check into a site and follow lots of linked pages. Some sites list those links in what is called a 'breadcrumb trail'. Try to create these for topics – they start with the overall idea, and move towards smaller and smaller detail. A bit like thought-mapping, but going along a line rather than using a large space. It is a topic tick list, really. For example:

Evil – meaning – example – how it started – defending God – responding to it

You can then use this trail to check how much you know. So, for example, you might be confident that you know what 'evil' means, can give some examples, and know the problems caused by it and how people respond. But, 'how it started' – not so sure. You know you need to check your notes and learn that more thoroughly.

Revision tip 2 – Flashcards

Make a set of flashcards and get someone to test your knowledge regularly with them. Put images and words on to the cards, such as examples of evil/suffering to classify, or words to define, or religious arguments to defend God. Someone holds up a flashcard and you talk about it. For example, a picture of evil is shown, you say 'evil'. Take it a step further, and justify or explain everything you say – if you can get into the habit of always doing this, you will do it automatically in the exam, and will boost your marks.

Revision tips that are not just hot air!

This page contains a number of ideas that you could try, and which would help you to revise. They are phrased in terms of this topic – but you can use them in any (and in your other subjects).

Revision tip 3 – Get visual

Collect pictures of as many of the things you study as you can. A picture with a caption sticks better in many people's heads than just writing. Then you can think of the image in the exam and it will help you to remember. For example, pictures that help you to remember why God allows suffering.

Revision tip 4 – Ballpark marking

You've done a test. Before it is marked, ask your teacher to return your test paper. They can then tell you exactly what the marks were for in each question, and you can judge your answers using this. When you get your marked test paper back, compare your guesstimate with your real mark. This makes you analyse your work more than you would if you just got it back marked, because you have to work out what your answer is worth. This means you understand better where you went wrong and how to improve. It means you pick up better techniques – which always means better marks.

Revision tip 5 – Time tests

Time tests are good for improving your timing, as well as strengthening your knowledge and technique. Here's a set of questions. Give yourself 25 minutes – no books.

1 Explain, using examples, the difference between evil and suffering. (3 marks)
2 **Nothing good comes out of suffering.** Do you agree? Explain your opinion. (3 marks)
3 Explain how the problem of evil and suffering causes problems for religious believers. (6 marks)
4 **You cannot solve the problem of evil and suffering.** Do you agree with this view? Give reasons for your answer, showing you have thought about more than one point of view. (6 marks)

Topic Four Immortalilty

What does this word mean?

It isn't about right and wrong – so don't make that mistake in the exam! It is to do with death, or rather not being dead, not ever. To be immortal is to never die, to live forever. Sound good?

Why is immortality important?

Perhaps it is more a case of the idea of an afterlife being important, and from that – if there is an afterlife – it must be forever. Belief in an afterlife is really important in all religions, whether it is a case of heaven or hell, or a birth into a new life in this world (**reincarnation**). For those believing in heaven and hell, the fact that they believe in God proves to them that there must be an afterlife – after all, God must live somewhere, and is himself **eternal**! The other thing that makes the idea of an afterlife attractive is that all the bad stuff you face in this life, all the times you didn't get what you deserved – you get compensated or rewarded for in an afterlife. Think about it, no matter how bad life gets, you can still have a great life to come, because God will make everything fine – and it will be forever.

This topic is about the whole idea of **immortality**. Have a look at these questions and try to answer them:

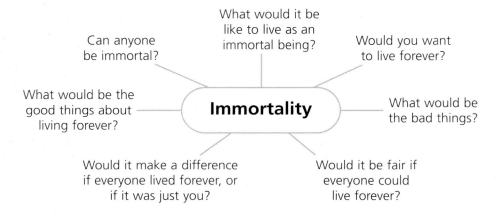

These questions are all quite easy to talk about, but quite tough at the same time. If you just had a chat about them, and came up with some ideas and some 'buts', give yourself a pat on the back – you've just been philosophising! We need to look at all these ideas for this course and, obviously, what some people have said to answer these questions.

So, before we explore what immortality might be, we need to get an idea of what death is. Any ideas? Which of these do you think counts as being dead?

They are all right in a way – each suggests death, though the heart can start again, as can breathing, and responses can be non-existent temporarily. The last sign is brain activity – and if there is none, it is an indication of death.

Okay, you are dead – how can you be immortal if you die? Or is death the step into immortality?

Stop breathing   **No responses**

Heart stops   **No brain activity**

Now you have thought about death and immortality

Mind, body and soul

Let's take it back a step. Before we talk about death and living forever, what are we? You see, what counts as us will have a big effect on what could live on – and whether we'd want it to.

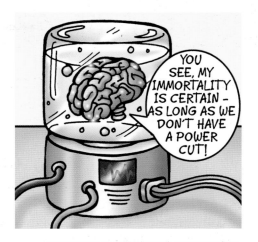

YOU SEE, MY IMMORTALITY IS CERTAIN – AS LONG AS WE DON'T HAVE A POWER CUT!

Will it be our mind? Have you ever heard someone say 'I'm going out of my mind…'? What do they mean by this? Your mind is the thing that does all the thinking, the thing that makes your personality what it is, like a big virtual storage box that is your essence. It isn't something we can cut someone open to find, but we all think we have one. Could this be the bit that is immortal?

What is going to continue?
Which bit of us will live forever?

Will we be able to just keep living in the body we have? We all have a body and it is how people recognise us (isn't it?) It is what makes us get from point a to point b, and is needed for anything physical. So surely we would need a body if we had to live forever…wouldn't we?

What about our **soul**? What is that? Maybe it is what makes us more than just our body. There's a difference between saying 'I left the room' and 'My body left the room', don't you think? It is a bit more of a spiritual idea than 'mind', which seems a bit scientific and clinical.

The idea of the body and soul as being separate but linked entities is called **dualism**. Many people believe we are a combination of the things mentioned on this page. However, given we can't prove the existence of the soul, that is a problem for belief in dualism.

Task

With a partner, explore the ideas of what might continue, and what the good and bad things about each might be. This will help you with the next stage of your thinking about this topic. Here are some questions to get you started:

- Do you need a physical place to go to so that you can live forever?
- If you cut a body open, you can't find the mind or soul – do they exist?
- If we have a soul, does everything else?
- How can someone still recognise me if they knew me at school, but I died when I was 90?
- Do I want to live forever if I am just my mind, or my soul, or my body?
- Are you still 'you' if any of those three elements is missing?
- Is there another option of what could live forever?

The Basics

1 What is meant by 'immortality'?
2 What are the 'mind', 'body' and 'soul'? What are the differences?
3 Explain which of the three options for immortality you prefer, and which you like/believe the least.
4 **It is impossible for our bodies to live forever.** Do you agree? Explain your answer, showing you have thought about more than one point of view.

Now you have thought about what makes us 'us'

What might count as life after death? ...Reincarnation

To find out more about **life after death**, let's ask our resident experts Count Dracula and Ned 'the Head'.

My guess is that we are *reincarnated*. Hindus and Sikhs believe this, and I've talked to many great thinkers in my lifetime. So here is how it goes – we are each made up of body and soul. Hindus call this the **atman**. The soul is like our true essence, the real us. Our body is like a vehicle that the soul lives in. When the body dies, the soul is released and then born again into another lifetime. How wonderful or awful those lives are is all based on how good or bad we were. If I am a terrible person in my life, then I will have to suffer through many lifetimes to make up for it. The good behaviour adds up and the bad behaviour adds up – then decides the state of our next lifetime (or next few). Karmic justice, some call it. This all means that each person is the sum of many lifetimes, and probably has many more to live through – until they are fit to be reunited with God. Each lifetime is a learning and development experience – the more you learn, the fewer you need.

Nah, I don't like that at all! Why don't people remember all these lives if they have them? Why can't everybody speak loads of languages, or be good at loads of different things? And another thing, if we all just keep getting reborn, why is the world's population going up and up? There seem to be too many people born for the ones who are dying to be reincarnated. And where's the proof?

NED THE HEAD

Well, if we remembered all our lives I think we'd go mad. It's bad enough when you've lived a life of hundreds of years – like me! What would we learn – probably how to cheat the system! And people *do* remember – they get hypnotised, and also there's a meditation you can do. Anyway, I like the idea of everything getting evened out over time – too many people get away with bad things in one lifetime.

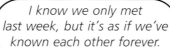

I know we only met last week, but it's as if we've known each other forever.

You Decide

1 What do we mean by 'reincarnation'?
2 What reasons could you give to support reincarnation, using what Dracula said and your own thoughts?
3 What reasons could you give against this idea, using what Ned said and your own thoughts?

...Memories

To find out more about life after death, let's ask our resident experts Count Dracula and Ned 'the Head'.

My idea is this. Our bodies just rot, don't they? Don't see how they can carry on. Even if they did, I wouldn't want that – you'd be old and wrinkly, get ill, bits would fall off. Not to mention that you couldn't go through walls or fly or anything, because everything that limits humans limits them because of their bodies.

So, actually, I don't think our bodies carry on. There's no proof that there is a soul. When has a doctor ever found one? Ever heard of a soul transplant? Didn't think so! So there's none of that either.

That leaves – nothing really! So I think we live after death in other people's *memories*. There are so many people you have met, or will meet in the future, and they all get a memory of you that they take with them. Families cherish these memories. Think of all the historical people we still remember – even when we didn't meet or know them. So, that's it for me – memories.

Not convinced at all, my transparent friend! I agree about the body and all that, but it's not really us living again if someone else is controlling a memory. What if they remember wrongly? What if they only had a bad memory to remember? Worst of all, what if you were little Mr Nobody? How long are you going to be remembered? Yeah, we all remember Henry VIII, but nobody remembers the maid who had to clean his bedpan, do they?! Nothing personal, Ned, but your idea is nothing personal!

Well, there is more proof of people from memories than physical proof. How many ghosts have you seen? How many times did you see a soul go by? How many times did you think of someone else – someone long gone? It's up to us to make sure everybody has good memories of us – that could be our goal in life.

You Decide

1 How do we live after death in this explanation?
2 What reasons could you give to support this theory, using what Ned said and your own thoughts?
3 What reasons could you give against this idea, using what Dracula said and your own thoughts?
4 What is your opinion of this idea? Is it a strong argument, or not? Is it reasonable to believe this or not? Explain why.

...Rebirth

To find out more about life after death, let's ask our resident experts Frank Junior and the Mummy.

I'm going to go with a **rebirth** theory myself. It's like reincarnation – you live lifetime after lifetime. However, it's not exactly the same 'you' that is reborn because each lifetime changes you a bit. So there isn't a permanent soul in the sense of a fixed unchanging thing. There's a sort of ever-changing soul-thing. Buddhists call this the **Anatta** (not soul). See, I don't think we stay the same – every experience changes us a bit. Can you really say you are exactly the same in every respect as you were this morning? Didn't think so!

I like the idea of things getting evened out across time, and having lots of chances to learn and develop so, to me, many lifetimes makes the most sense.

So I think that our Anatta gets reborn into many lifetimes, always changing but each time learning and developing. Eventually, it is pure enough or clever enough to stop living these lives – let's face it they are a bit of a drag at times!

Don't like that, Frankie-boy! How can something be reborn if it isn't the same as what died? Changes make it a different thing, so I reckon that cancels out the idea of another life. Where's your proof of anything other than our bodies anyway? If it isn't physical, it just isn't anything. Why don't people remember these other lives or bits of them at least? You've not thought about this hard enough.

We can't remember all our lives – it would be too much. Plus, that would get in the way of our development in this life. We'd be too busy dreaming and thinking of the past to get on with making sure we had a positive experience this time around. Anyway, millions of Buddhists can't be wrong!

You Decide

1 What do we mean by 'rebirth'?
2 How is rebirth different from reincarnation?
3 Ever-changing, non-permanent self, or permanent soul – which do you prefer, and why?
4 What reasons could you give to support this theory, using what Frank Junior said and your own thoughts?
5 What reasons could you give against this idea, using what the Mummy said and your own thoughts?

...Resurrection

To find out more about life after death, let's ask our resident experts Frank Junior and the Mummy.

I think the Christians got it right. I like the sound of **resurrection**. You die, and then wake up and still have a physical body. How can anyone get around without a body? I can't just 'think' myself to somewhere else, I have to go. We need our bodies so we can do stuff. Back to the Christians, they think that at the end of time God will wake people up from their graves, and they will be bodily resurrected. The good ones will go to heaven, which is a really top place – lots to enjoy (so we definitely need that body!) There is a bit of a debate about whether God will wake up the bad ones and parcel them off to hell, or just not bother to wake them up. So, my money is on a bodily resurrection at the end of time. Heaven, here I come!

Don't be ridiculous! Bodily resurrection, indeed! How will that happen? How can a body that has rotted to nothing hundreds of years ago be resurrected? And another thing, what happens if I died as a decrepit old man? Do I really want that body to live again with all its aches, pains and illnesses? Think I'd prefer my younger athletic self, actually! Then again, whatever body I had, it'd start to decay and get old again. It might get diseased or damaged. And where's heaven? A physical body needs a physical home. Never seen heaven through a telescope! Face it; this idea of yours has too many problems!

Such a negative attitude! You forgot about God. If God can create the world and God can do all the miracles, then there isn't a problem. Christians say resurrection of the body, and I am sure God can fix all the problems before they even start. Just got to trust in God's word on this one – God knows best.

You Decide

1 What do we mean by 'resurrection'?
2 What reasons could you give to support this theory, using what the Mummy said and your own thoughts?
3 What reasons could you give against this idea, using what Frank Junior said and your own thoughts?
4 **People accept what their religion tells them without thinking the ideas through.** What do you think? Explain your opinion.

...A legacy

To find out more about life after death, let's ask our resident experts Tiny and the Professor.

I was asked how we can live after our death, and all I can come up with is that it is because of what we did. Take me for example – the most feared dinosaur ever. You only need to see my skeleton to be afraid, very afraid. Anyway, I ruled the earth, and my dominance is my legacy – you humans copy me all the time. People like Leonardo da Vinci, well, he's amazing – his art, his ideas, his books. They are his gift to the world, his legacy, and he lives on through them. What about the Great Wall in China – the legacy of Emperor Qin Shi Huang? You can see that from the moon, you know. Everyone leaves a 'footprint' whether it is small, big or huge – everyone has the chance to make that contribution, and that is their immortality.

Tsk, tsk! I see the logic, but I don't like it. Really it means I don't live on – my work does. Just because my children have my genes, doesn't mean that they are me, does it? What if someone else gets credited with my legacy – does that mean I don't get immortality for it? Qin Shi Huang's wall is long gone – it's everybody else's that we see, but we don't remember them! Come to think of it, how many people even know of Qin Shi Huang? I want to live again – my life's experiments have been geared towards making that happen – sorry, but your idea just doesn't do it for me!

Your legacy doesn't have to be worldwide – I'm sure a few billion Chinese can tell you about Qin! Anyway, you have no proof for anything else – despite your life's work! At least this one is certain, even if it is a bit impersonal. I'm going to stick with my idea.

You Decide

1 How do we live after death in this explanation?
2 Is it really 'life'? Explain why.
3 Think of what your legacy would be, or what you'd like it to be. Ask a partner what they think of your legacy, and how long lasting it would be.
4 What is your opinion of this idea? Is it a strong argument? Is it reasonable to believe this? Explain why.
5 If your legacy only lasts a few generations, is it really immortality? Explain your opinion.

Now you know about theories of immortality and their problems

Why do people want to be immortal?

Remember 'immortality' is everlasting life, life eternal, never dying. You have thought about the different ways we could live forever, and some of the problems with those ideas. You probably came up with more reasons than you met in this book too.

> Would you like to live forever? Why?
> What would you do if you lived forever?

Task

Read the following statements and pick out the reasons why the speakers want immortality. Do any match your ideas?

1 I want to live forever, so I can see how my family develops and goes on.

2 There is so much to learn and so little time. I want to travel to so many places and see so many cultures. I can't do it all in one lifetime.

3 I want to see history made, see civilisations rise and fall – I need to live forever for that.

4 My religion promises me I can live forever. Immortality would prove I was right to choose that religion.

5 I am frightened of death, so I never want to die.

6 I want to beat the laws of nature – and living forever is exactly that.

7 I enjoy life so much; I never want it to end.

8 There's never a good time to die, so I'd prefer not to. There's always something to finish off, or something to check out.

Now check out these comments – they are all reasons why people might not want to live forever:

A Very bad boy in this life – got away with it, but might not next time!

B Don't want a real body – it'll get old and hurt. Too ugly!

C I was bored to tears in this life. More of that? No thanks!

D If I believe in nothing and there is nothing, I won't be disappointed!

E What if my next life is as bad as this was?

F One life is enough for anyone.

You Decide

1 Give three reasons why some people would like there to be immortality.
2 Give three reasons why some people would not want immortality.
3 **It is silly to believe in life after death.** Do you agree? Give reasons and explain your answer, showing you have thought about more than one point of view. Refer to religious arguments in your answer.

Now you have thought about why people do/don't want life after death

'Proving' life after death

People choose to believe or not to believe that there is life after death. They are influenced in that by their religion, their wishes, their upbringing and their experiences, as well as many other reasons. They 'choose' to believe because they can't know for certain – there is no proof (except for a legacy or in memories, but both have their own limited lifespan).

Let's look at some of the evidence to believe…

Holy books

The holy books of all religions tell us that there will be life after death, and life eternal. If you believe in and follow a religion, you accept its teachings as fact. So you believe that there is eternal life because the book says so – that is your proof. For example, in the Gospel of John, it says 'For whosoever believes in him [Jesus] shall not die but have everlasting life'. Simple – believe in Jesus, live forever. Christianity is based on this.

The blobs on the photos are called orbs. People who believe in ghosts think they are evidence of the spirit world.

Ghost experience

Lots of people claim to have seen ghosts. Lots of people claim to see the same ghost. There is a huge interest in ghosts – whether they exist, and what they really are – there is even a satellite channel for this subject! There appears to be plenty of photo and film evidence too. So seeing a ghost – a sense of a presence of someone dead, or a non-solid image of them (like a film projection) – is proof. Some ghosts are just there, as if they are recordings of people or events that play over and over again. Some ghosts seem to interact with humans – in good and bad ways – suggesting that they have a conscience and some control.

Channelling

This is mediumship or **spiritualism**. Some people claim to be able to contact the dead and speak with them to get messages. There is a whole religious movement based on this – the Spiritualist Church. We call the people who can 'talk to the dead' **mediums**. Often their message is so real and accurate that the listeners can only believe they have spoken with their loved one. Let's face it, spiritualism has been going strong throughout human existence, and the Spiritualist churches have strong congregations. So when the medium gives messages from *the other side*, some believe this proves life after death.

Near-death experiences

People all over the world have experienced these. Basically, the person 'dies', but has an experience that they can recall very clearly, and then they come back to life. That experience is almost always the same – regardless of where in the world they live, and what their life experiences have been. It usually involves moving through a tunnel of light, meeting people at the end (people who they knew/loved but are now dead, and/or religious figures), and then being pulled back into their body and life. The experience is blissful, but the return often painful, as they have to go back to feeling the pain of a damaged body. Doctors can say for certain that they died in the period they were having this experience.

Revelation

You already know that revelation is God revealing himself. So how does this prove immortality? Well, it is linked to all the rest of the teachings of the faith. If you can meet God, then the religion you follow is right, and all of its teachings are too. There is an eternal, powerful being, and that being must be able to fulfil the promises of eternal life.

Research Task

Go internet surfing and find out more on these topics. The exam is unlikely to want more detail – but it's really interesting! Research near-death experiences from different cultures. You could watch a few programmes like *Most Haunted*, or check out the 'Paranormal Channel', or watch some of the many TV series based on someone who claims they can talk to/see dead people, like *Medium*, or *Ghost Whisperer*. You could build up a file of evidence to present to the class.

The Basics

1 Why is there evidence but no proof of life after death?
2 What evidence could be offered for life after death? For each type of evidence you give, write a couple of sentences to explain it.
3 What do you think is the strongest evidence? Why?
4 What is the weakest evidence? Why?
5 Does this convince you that there is life after death? Explain your opinion.

Life after death – there's no such thing!

It's back to that simple point – there is no conclusive proof, so people have a choice of whether they believe or not. Some people are just sceptical and will only believe when they experience something for themselves, and even then they have to have no other explanation. So what's the evidence against it?

If there is so much evidence, why do people still not believe?

No, no, no…

No proof

None of the sightings of ghosts can be proved. There are always other answers as to why something happened – even when it is on tape. So it never gets beyond being evidence to be a proof – which can't be argued with.

Other explanations

In the case of **near-death experiences**, scientists have a theory that our brain is programmed to make us hallucinate to make death easier mentally. So everyone has the same 'programmed' experience, it's just that we only know about it from those who are revived. Although we could say they have life after death – because technically they did die – it isn't immortality.

Dodgy witnesses

Many of the witnesses of these events are discredited. Maybe they were brought up to interpret things in a certain way, so their explanation is biased. Maybe they are out to make some money. Many sceptics rule things out as evidence or proof simply because of who mentioned/experienced them.

Science

If you heard a ghost speak on a windy night, how can you be sure it wasn't the breeze? If you saw light anomalies (orbs), wasn't it dust or insects instead? There are often other explanations, which science can provide, or tries to.

Disbelief and atheism

Given that lots of the beliefs are tied up in a bunch of religious beliefs, many people choose not to believe in ideas of life after death. Without personal experience, they have nothing to encourage them to think that way.

The Basics

1   What evidence is there against life after death? For each type you give, explain yourself.
2   **People don't disprove life after death, they just argue against the people or their experience.** Do you agree? Explain your reasons.

Now you have thought about evidence against life after death

What the religions believe about life after death

We've mentioned religious beliefs, so let's quickly see what they are on this subject.

Buddhism

Buddhists believe in rebirth. There is no permanent soul, rather a mix of ever-changing skandhas – emotions, feelings, intelligence and so on. After the death of the body, this mix fuses with an egg and sperm at conception. The thoughts, actions and intentions of each life shape the quality of the next. The goal is to achieve enlightenment, and stop being reborn.

Christianity ✝

Christians believe in the physical resurrection of the body. At death, the body (with soul) waits until Judgement Day. Catholics call this Purgatory. At judgement, the person faces God and Jesus to evaluate their deeds. If they were good in life, they go to heaven, which is paradise and wonderful forever. If they were bad, they go to hell for eternal punishment.

Judaism ☰

Judaism focuses on this life rather than the next. Some teachings mention a heavenly place. Jews talk of the 'world to come', which is when the Messiah will come to rule the earth in peace. This is life after death because the dead will be woken to live through this time.

Religious teachings

Hinduism ॐ

Hindus believe in reincarnation. Their atman (soul) lives through many lifetimes, each one shaped by the thoughts, words and actions of their past lifetime(s). Its goal is to achieve enlightenment and become one with the **Ultimate Reality**, so stopping being reincarnated.

Sikhism ☬

Sikhs believe in reincarnation. The soul is born into many lifetimes, whose quality is decided by the words, thoughts and deeds of the previous lifetime(s). The point of each life is to serve and worship God, so that eventually the soul can be reunited with God (waheguru) and stop being reincarnated.

Islam ☪

Muslims believe in resurrection. At death, the body waits in the grave (barzakh) and sees the events of its life. This can be quick or very slow and painful. On Judgement Day, people are sorted according to their beliefs and actions. The wicked are cast into hell; the truly good go straight to paradise. All others cross As-Sirat Bridge, carrying the book of their deeds (sins make it heavier). The bridge is sharp, and so they are purified from sin before going to paradise.

The Basics

1. Choose two religions. Describe, in your own words, what they believe about life after death.
2. **Believing in life after death affects how we behave now**. Do you agree? Give reasons for your answer, showing you have thought about more than one point of view.

Exam tips

One of the common problems in exams is when candidates don't match their answer to the question. That's not to say they get it wrong – of course, at times they do exactly that! No, there are other ways they get it wrong. Can you spot what is wrong in the answers to the following exam questions?

1 Explain some of the evidence for life after death. (4 marks)

Answer 1

There is no such thing as life after death. There is no proof because the people who see ghosts can't be trusted. No one has ever come back from the dead to prove to everyone there is another life. I think it is just something people believe to make this life a bit more bearable.

Answer 2

Seeing ghosts, having a near-death experience, talking to the dead through mediums, and what it says in your religion all prove there is life after death.

2 Give three reasons why some people believe in life after death. (3 marks)

Answer 3

Firstly, their religion tells them there is life after death. Jesus said that anyone could have eternal life if they believed in him. He also said that he would meet his disciples again in paradise. Secondly, they might have met a ghost. I saw my gran in my bedroom late at night one night. We had a chat and she went. I thought she must have come over for something (she lives in London and I live in Liverpool). The next day my mum told me gran had died in the night of a heart attack. I saw her ghost, so I know there is life after death. Thirdly, they might go to a medium and be told stuff that the medium couldn't have known. So then they believe there is another life.

Answer 4

They believe it because it makes them feel better about their life now – things will be better after, see. They don't want to die either, so if they believe in life after death, they won't.

3 **Bodily resurrection is the most likely way to live after death.** Do you agree? Give reasons for your answer, showing you have thought about more than one point of view.   (6 marks)

Answer 5

Yes, because that is what Christianity says. The whole religion teaches that, it's even in a prayer. Plus, we recognise each other through what we look like, so we'd need our bodies after we die.

But I'd also ask that if we do get resurrected, what will the body be like? It will get old again or start falling to bits. Our body can't last forever, so that doesn't make sense really. And what about meeting people who didn't know us when we were old and died – would they recognise us? Who'd want to have a baby's body – that can't do anything for itself – for eternity?

Answer 6

I think the idea we'd have a body again is stupid. Science says I have a full new body of cells every seven years, so which body will it be? What if I gave my kidneys, eyes, liver, heart, cornea, and anything else they could take after I died? Those bits would be in someone else's body – so who would get them next time around? If I were them, I wouldn't want my old bits back – they'd be rubbish. Also, your body is physical, so it gets bashed about, and damaged, ill and old. Scientifically, it can't last forever. And finally, where would it go? God would have to make another planet (or loads of them actually) to fit everybody on.

Another view might be to say that there are other options other than resurrection. We could be reincarnated or reborn. So our soul lives through lots of different lifetimes to get cleverer, purer or whatever. Then it can be back with God or be enlightened. More than half the world believes that, so they might be right.

So what did you spot?

Which one(s) wrote more than they needed?

Which one(s) didn't explain when they needed to?

Which one(s) answered the wrong question?

Which one(s) didn't follow the correct technique to get better marks?

Exam Tips

Here's the commentary and tips for you to turn those answers into much better ones:

Answer 1 The question wants to know evidence FOR, but the answer gives evidence AGAINST. 0 marks! So, give three pieces of evidence, and explain each one, perhaps giving an example each time.

Answer 2 Hasn't explained at all. Use the evidence in the answer and explain each.

Answer 3 They have explained everything, when they only needed to give three short phrases/words. A simple list sorts this question.

Answer 4 Gave two answers not three – give the right number to get full marks.

Answer 5 Gives two sides and mentions religion – so far, so good. However, nothing is developed/explained and it needs to be for the higher marks. So, explain the points made – sometimes examples are the best form of explanation.

Answer 6 This says it gives two views, but actually it doesn't. Really it only gives one view, just two versions of it. For these questions, you MUST both AGREE and DISAGREE to get the top marks.

Topic Five Miracles

PLANE CRASHES – ALL 73 SURVIVE

GAS MAIN BLAST KILLS ENTIRE FAMILY

CANCER VICTIM RECOVERS – 'THANK GOD FOR THIS 1 IN 10 MIRACLE' SAYS FAMILY

FLOOD DAMAGE LEADS TO PRIMARY SCHOOL COLLAPSE – ONLY 7 SURVIVE

THOUSANDS FLOCK TO SEE IMAGE OF JESUS ON WINDOW

MASS MURDERER CAUGHT BEFORE HE COULD KILL HIS FINAL VICTIM

MAN CLAIMS TO HAVE VISIONS OF GOD WHEN HE HAS SEIZURES

WOMAN LIFTS CAR OFF HER BABY'S PRAM AFTER IT ROLLS BACK ON TO IT

> *Which of these are miracles? Can you say why you would label any of them as miracles? If you were the lucky one in each case, would you think it was a miracle? How would you feel if you were the family of the unlucky ones – still a miracle?*

Funny things miracles. People have an idea of what counts as a miracle; they can often give characteristics of miracles and can usually give a real or made-up example. Sometimes people disagree about whether something is a miracle or not – not always because they don't believe in God.

For this topic, you need to be able to say what miracles are, and why they are called miracles. You also need to be able to say what miracles tell us about God, and what problems they cause for believers in God. You might also be asked about David Hume, who wrote a whole argument against anything being a miracle. These are all part of the course, so you could get asked questions about them.

First things first, let's get an idea of what we mean by that word 'miracle'.

Research Task

Carry out an internet search on the word 'miracle'.

1. How many sites could you check out that mention miracle?
2. Find five entirely different miracles, and make brief notes on them.
3. Print out pictures to back up your notes.
4. For each, say who claims it is a miracle and why they think that.
5. From these examples, write a definition of 'miracle'.

 Now you have thought about miracles

What do we mean by miracles?

Traditionally, miracles are events that seem impossible. They go against the **laws of nature** (the processes which science has shown nature operates through). They aren't something that could normally happen. They are extraordinary events.

> Using the headlines on page 58, which events come under these descriptions?

Also traditionally, miracles are events associated with God or some religious significance. They are seen as God answering prayers or helping. They are interpreted as revelations of God or some important religious figure.

> Using the headlines on page 58, which events come under these descriptions?

Finally, miracles are always good. God uses his power (omnipotence) to help because of his love for us (benevolence).

> Using the headlines on page 58, which events come under these descriptions?

Let's think about the events in those headlines. You have already talked about which ones are miracles, and why. As important as it is for an event to meet the three criteria above, it is also about people's interpretation of events. You see, for example, the families of those who survived the school that collapsed would probably say it was a miracle. I'll bet the families of the dead wouldn't! One person could have a vision of angels – their family might say it was a miracle, whilst they themselves didn't believe that. Different people see things in different ways.

Try this one – it is a real event.

Nev got injured at work. He got caught in the conveyor belt of an industrial shredder. The belt of the shredder snapped, so he didn't get dragged in, but he did have his arm snapped into pieces, and the nerves in his shoulder completely severed. He couldn't switch the machine off, but the belt snapping saved his life ('Miracle number one,' says his wife). In hospital after many tests, doctors announced that he would never be able to use his arm and hand again. He was paralysed. Several months of repeat testing confirmed this diagnosis. His wife prayed regularly, and had her friends and fellow Christians at church do the same; Nev isn't religious. Some ten months later – long after treatment has stopped, beyond painkillers – Nev gets a tingling in his fingers. He visits the doctor, who sends him for tests – there is life again. The unfixable has somehow mended itself. Today, he can use his arm and hand freely and like anyone else. His wife says this was miracle number two; Nev just shrugs, and says he is just lucky.

> Why does Nev's wife think this is a miracle?

> What does Nev think?

> What does this tell you about labelling events as miracles?

> If it isn't a miracle, what other explanation could there be?

Some miracles...in holy books

It is likely that the exam will want you to give some examples of miracles. Even if you aren't asked directly for an example, you can use them to develop points you make. Examples act as good explanations – remember that – because they show the examiner you know what you are talking about. The exam can't ever ask you for a miracle story from one specific religion, so you just need to know some examples.

Examples from scripture and tradition

There are a number of stories of Jesus performing miracles in the New Testament. He does different kinds of miracles – sometimes healing people, sometimes doing an 'impossible' thing. Let's look at one of each.

A healing miracle

In the Gospel of Mark is the story of Blind Bartimaeus – well, blind until he met Jesus, that is! Bartimaeus – blind from birth – heard that Jesus was coming through his town. He waited by the road until he could hear the crowd and then called for help from Jesus. Jesus heard his shouts and – impressed with the faith Bartimaeus had shown in Jesus' ability to heal him – healed his blindness.

An 'impossible' thing

In the same Gospel, Jesus was talking to crowds of people. This was quite common – and it's not just the Bible that says Jesus was a really charismatic speaker to whom crowds flocked for his words, historians of the time inform us of that too. So, on this particular day, Jesus talked for a long time. They were all in a quite deserted place – it was far from any town. His disciples realised the crowd (of 5000) would be hungry, so should be sent away immediately before they started to ask for food – there was none. The only food to be found was five loaves and two fish. Jesus blessed and broke the bread and fish, and just kept blessing and breaking. In the end, everyone ate their fill, and there were twelve baskets of fragments left over.

The Basics

1 Why are these two events considered 'miracles'?
2 How do they show the qualities of the miracles we encountered on page 59?
3 If you had been a witness of either of these events, what would you have thought? Explain your answer.
4 For one of the stories, draw a cartoon strip; for the other write an eye-witness statement. This gives you two miracle stories to use in the exam.
5 **Jesus did miracles because God gave him the power.** Do you agree? Give reasons for your answer, showing you have thought about more than one point of view.

Now you have learnt two religious examples of a miracle

...in history

If you did an internet search for 'miracles in history', you would get pages and pages of websites. Many, many events are recorded as miracles. It might seem easy to find a different solution now, e.g. visions could be migraines. However, there are still many that seem too miraculous to be anything but a miracle.

A trip through Christian history provides many people who were said to perform miracles. Augustine of Hippo (354–430 CE) wrote a book called *City of God*, which listed many miracles. There are long descriptions of every kind of healing of humans and animals that you can think of, and examples of casting out of demons and other kinds of miracles. History tells us of miracles before and after that time.

Lourdes

Bernadette Soubirous was fourteen in 1858. She lived in Lourdes, but often went to the countryside around her town. One day, at a grotto far from her home, she claimed she saw a beautiful woman. She saw her eighteen times, and the woman told her that she was the 'Immaculate Conception', meaning

she was the Virgin Mary – mother of Jesus. Bernadette told people who began to visit. Spring water from the grotto was believed to have healing powers. Many went to be cured of illnesses. About 5,000,000 people a year go there now. Not all go to be cured, but records of miracles come in from Lourdes all the time.

Other religious miracles

Actually, it isn't just Christian history that claims miracles. People of all religions claim miracles have happened at many of their holy sites. Hindus bathe in the Ganges, and believe miracles happen. Muslims will visit the tombs of Muhammad and other important early Muslims to ask for miracles and cures.

In Goa, India, the body of St Francis Xavier is on view. He is credited with converting more people to Christianity than anyone other than St Paul. When he died, his body was buried and then dug up and moved to a different country several times, but it has not decomposed – in over 300 years! He is minus one of his toes though, because a woman who came to pay her respects to the body bit it off as a keepsake and as a talisman for miracles. That was when you could walk past the body in an open coffin once a year in a memorial ceremony – they stopped it after she did that! Bits of dead saints and holy people are often thought to cause miracles – there are lots of stories in history about that.

The Basics

1 Why do you think some people disbelieve 'historical miracles'?
2 Find out about two historical miracles – a healing one, and a non-healing one. Why are these miracles? Why are they believable as miracles?
3 **Modern science shows historical miracles as not miracles at all.** What do you think? Explain your opinion.

Now you have thought about historical miracles

...from experience

Whether you believe in them or not, people claim to experience miracles every day somewhere in the world. Let's check some out…

In September 1995 and again in 2006, statues of Ganesha were said to be drinking milk. This was happening in Hindu temples all over the world. Reporters flocked to the temples, knocking worshippers (who also flocked to the temples) out of their way to get pictures and 'disprove' the miracles. They wanted to prove it was all a fake. They failed! No one could reasonably explain how and why the statues of the elephant-headed god were drinking the milk. No one could work out where it was disappearing to – because it disappeared in their plain view, and there was no trickery with hidden pipes or spaces.

William Kent was put into a wheelchair after a serious motorcycle accident. He should never have walked again, and the damage to the rest of his body was also extensive, including leaving him diabetic. He took up shooting and entered contests for disabled athletes. He went to the Seoul Paralympics (1988) to represent the USA. In three years he won many medals, and set many world records. In 2000, he felt that he should visit a

particular town, and once there a particular church service. In that service he felt compelled to try to stand and then to walk. He did both – for the first time in over fifteen years. His diabetes was also cured. He says God did this, and that he felt God's healing power doing it – a miracle.

In 1982, Angela Cavello heard her neighbour yelling for her. She went out to see her own son pinned under a car he had been doing some mechanics on. He was unconscious and the life was being squeezed out of him. She yelled for the neighbour to get the ambulance and rushed to the car. She gripped the car and lifted it enough for her son to be able to be pulled out. She held that car up about six inches from the ground on her own for at least five minutes. Now, she is a woman of five feet in height and average build – how did she do it? She claims a miracle, simple as.

The Basics

1   Describe the three miracles on this page.
2   Why do people link God to each?
3   What problems are caused by believing God made any of these happen?

So, who performs miracles?

What a strange question! *What's your answer?*

Someone who is religious might say God does. But if I go to a healer and they heal me by laying hands on me – did they do it, or did God? What if I go to a healer and don't get healed – does that mean God was busy, or that they have no power, or that I didn't deserve it? And that is a whole other problem!

Angela Cavello lifted that car. She was the one to exert the energy and lift what she shouldn't have been able to for five minutes. Did God act through her? Did he temporarily give her special powers? A sceptic might say that if it was God, why did he not help every person who got trapped under a car? The same day Angela was saving her teenage son, a baby in its pushchair was crushed to death under its mum's car after she left the handbrake off. Scientists would say that in times of extreme stress, some humans gain special powers – it is part of how we are made. That is how science explains Angela's miracle.

Many miracles seem not to have had a human involved – a miracle recovery from a supposedly terminal brain cancer, for example. The doctors tell the patient there is nothing more they can do. The patient chooses to cease medication. At their next monthly check-up, instead of finding them near to death the doctor finds no trace of the tumour. It's called *spontaneous regression,* and basically means that medical science has no explanation for a real event. No one did anything to the patient except let them go away to die. Did God fix it? No one else could have done.

Or were all of these just random events in nature? Things that could happen to anyone at any time – just a case of very good luck.

You need to have some ideas about who performs miracles – humans, God, or are they just random acts of nature? You need an answer to this, along with reasons why – better candidates always explain themselves.

Can humans perform miracles?

The Basics

1 Using examples, explain who or what causes miracles.
2 Why do you think people attribute these kinds of events to God?
3 What explanation can you give for why God doesn't perform a miracle in every situation?
4 **God must exist if miracles do.** What do you think? Explain your opinion.

Miraculous evidence

Read these events – what evidence is there, and what could we conclude about each?

What evidence can we get from miraculous events?

A boy wanders on to a rail track just as a train is due. The train roars towards him, and suddenly the driver has a heart attack and dies. As the driver slumps, he releases the 'dead man's handle'. The train slows and stops – just in front of the boy. The boy is left unhurt.

A man wakes to find his house in flames. He manages to grab his baby daughter from her cradle and with no other option leaps from the third floor room. He lands. His daughter is safe; he escapes with a sprained ankle.

After many different doctors diagnosed Sarah infertile, she gave up trying to have a baby. Five years later, having had no medical treatment, she gave birth to twin sons.

A man has to attend a business trip in New York. He has a strange feeling about it and, even though it is all organised through his PA, he asks her to rearrange for the week before. He goes on his trip, and very successfully meets with business colleagues in their offices in the World Trade Centre. On the same day, at the time he would have been there just one week later, a plane rips through the floor on which the offices of that business were situated. Everyone dies.

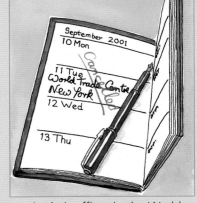

You may now be using the word 'coincidence' – events that happen alongside each other and often complement each other, or collide to make things much worse. These are random, with no planning – like using a cash machine when it is issuing double money because it has been wrongly set, or going to the bank on the day it gets robbed by armed raiders. So are these events coincidence or miracles?

The Basics

1 For each event, decide whether it is a miracle or a coincidence? Explain why.
2 How could each be seen to be a miracle?
3 Do any persuade you that miracles happen? Why?

Learning about God

If we believe these events are caused by God – either directly or indirectly – then they must tell us something about the nature of God. They must give us a glimpse into God's personality and characteristics.

> For each of the following events, what are we learning about God?

BOLTON WOMAN CUTS AUBERGINE TO FIND NAME OF GOD WRITTEN IN ITS SEEDS

FOUR YEAR OLD CURED OF LEUKAEMIA – PARENTS SPEAK OF TRAUMATIC MONTHS OF ILLNESS

MIRACULOUS HEALINGS HAPPEN EVERY WEEK AT ALPHA CENTRE CHURCH

CROWDS FLOCK TO SEE MIRACULOUS IMAGE OF VIRGIN MARY ON WINDOWS OF BUILDING

PILGRIMAGE TO MECCA SEES WOMAN HEALED OF LIFE-LONG ILLNESS

BOY STILL MEDITATING AFTER MONTHS WITHOUT FOOD OR WATER

You probably decided that God was good (benevolent) because he helped these people. He is immanent because he interfered in the world. He is powerful (omnipotent) because he can fix the impossible. He must also be clever to do that (omniscient). Plus, he has to be in existence still. In other words, these events describe a God who cares for his creation and can, and will, help it. You have already seen that people take miracles as proof of God's existence – here you can see why.

Let's play devil's advocate though! We could say the miracles are the silver lining on black clouds – most will have come at the end of a very stressful period. But can you see a black lining to these silver linings? What about all the other people in the same circumstances who didn't get the cure? And what's the point of putting a name in a vegetable – why not use the power to help/heal? Miracles are tricky issues – they have two very different interpretations. Many people think they cause more problems than they solve.

The Basics

1 If you were the recipient of these miracles, would they make you believe in God? Explain.
2 What does each miracle tell you about God?
3 **Miracles show God as cruel, unloving and unhelpful.** Do you agree? Give reasons for your answer, showing you have thought about more than one point of view.

David Hume on miracles

David Hume (1711–76) was a Scottish philosopher and sceptic. One of his many works was *Dialogues Concerning Natural Religion*, published in 1779 after his death. In this, he argues against miracles – that they simply don't exist. For the exam, you need to know the main points of Hume's argument. You will agree with some of them and, if you do, make sure you can express them for yourself, because those points will help you to answer questions about miracles in the exam. If you think Hume's point is not right, or has a problem, then remember this – it will be useful when you discuss his argument.

A wise man bases his belief on the evidence he has – more evidence means stronger belief.

If something has been seen before in nature, then it isn't a miracle. Miracles aren't part of nature, so should not be part of normal experience.

Miracles are not natural – the laws of nature are broken when a miracle happens.

Any witness statement has to be challenged. What is said has to be more believable than any other alternative before that statement can be accepted as valid.

Accounts of miracles in history have never been witnessed by enough people whose integrity and intelligence could not be in doubt. In other words, there has been something wrong with the witnesses of every miracle in history, so that their testimony is not credible.

Miracle 103   England

~~Miracle 104   Africa~~

~~Miracle 105   Arabia~~

Miracle 106   France

~~Miracle 107   China~~

Hume dismisses the claim for a miracle from any country not considered educated or civilised. When Hume was alive, this meant that only miracles in Europe (and not all of Europe) would count! He believed people from other countries knew too little science to be able to judge events properly.

Anyone who is religious is likely to exaggerate or misinterpret what they see. Some will even lie to further their religion! Their testimony must be discounted.

Hume has obviously discounted all chance of proving a miracle in these circumstances. However, he does describe a miracle at the tomb of Abbe Paris. He writes of many, many miracles happening there. He says there were many reliable witnesses who saw them and verified them. He says no one was able to prove any fraud or deceit, though they did try. He even says that the most suitable reason for these events was that they were miracles.

My head has stopped hurting

I can see!

So does this give Hume the proof of miracles he needs? NO – he still discounts them! He simply says it is impossible for so many miracles to happen at the same place to so many people. Of course, he didn't see any miracles for himself – and that might be the crucial point in his argument, though he doesn't say it. Actually, he would probably only believe what he himself saw; he didn't see them, so there must be another explanation. They weren't miracles (and neither was any other that claims to be).

So there you have it – Hume's argument against miracles. You might have decided that some of it was wrong or unfair (like discounting anyone's testimony if they were from another country or if they hadn't been highly educated). The course outline doesn't say that you have to pull Hume's argument apart – that's left for AS level. However, it might be appropriate in 'Do you agree?' questions, so think your ideas through and keep them in mind.

The Basics

1 Who was David Hume?
2 Write a checklist outlining whether or not something is a miracle according to Hume.
3 Do you think Hume gives us any good reasons to discount events as miracles? Explain your answer.
4 **Hume was never interested in proving miracles existed.** What do you think? Explain your opinion.

Now you know Hume's argument against miracles

Exam tips – improving exam performance

We are going to look at a couple of techniques for improving marks – these don't rely on what you have learnt. They are about *how* you tackle the exam questions.

Checking the paper

I know, all the teachers tell you millions of times *read the paper before you start*. Most people don't follow that advice. Those who do, often just skim through it without really taking any notice of it. *So, why bother checking?*

Do you panic before or in exams? Many do, and it affects their performance. How many times have you done a test, and afterwards swapped answers with friends. Then you realise you put the wrong thing for some questions – but you knew the right answer – doh!

Reading through the paper first can act as a calming exercise, reducing that panic/stress level. Make it part of your exam habit.

Another thing – take a highlighter into the exam. As you read the paper, highlight the key words in the questions. There are two sorts of key words – **command words**, which tell you what to do, like *Explain* and *Why*. Get those wrong and kiss goodbye to decent or even any marks. Then there are **trigger words**, which are the subject of the question. If the question is about evidence *for* miracles, don't write about evidence *against* them – you won't get any marks.

Checking your answers

When you have finished answering all the questions in an exam, what do you do? Teachers say: 'Smart people check their answers.' *Do you?* You do: excellent. BUT, *how* do you check your answers?

Most people read the question again, and then read their answer again. They think it is fine, then move on to the next question. They don't spot many changes or additions needed.

Here is a better way…

This is a much better way to check. Our brains are lazy and will just limit our ideas if we can read an answer. They take the route already followed, and so usually don't see a different idea.

Using this technique, your brain has to do some work. This way, your brain might give you new things to say, hence some more marks.

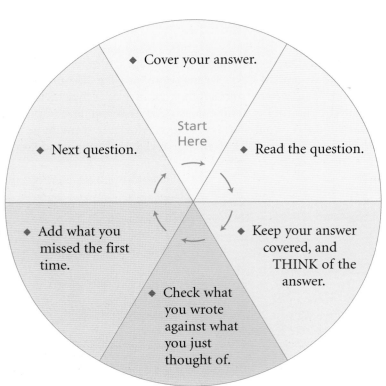

- Cover your answer.
- Read the question.
- Keep your answer covered, and THINK of the answer.
- Check what you wrote against what you just thought of.
- Add what you missed the first time.
- Next question.

Start Here

Let's try that technique

Have a look at these questions and answers. The *command* and *trigger* words are highlighted for you in the first question. *Can you spot them in the second?* Check the answers using the technique outlined on page 68. *Can you improve the answers?*

1 Using examples, explain what we mean by miracle. (3 marks)

Jodie's answer

Miracles are things that shouldn't happen – they are impossible. They are made by God. They are always good.

2 Humans can't perform miracles. What do you think? Explain your opinion. (3 marks)

Ashley's Answer

I agree – miracles are impossible. Ordinary people can't do them. They haven't got enough power.

3 Explain what religious believers learn of God from miracles. (4 marks)

Ahmed's Answer

God is loving. God loves the person helped very much. If he didn't, he wouldn't help them. For example, if I was dying of cancer, and I prayed to God for help, and God helped me, I would feel very honoured. I would know that God is loving and compassionate without reading it in the holy book.

4 Explain the argument against miracles. (4 marks)

Shaq's Answer

It says there are no miracles. You can't trust people who see a miracle. People get mistaken and see things in their mind that they think are real. We don't know all the science, so it could be natural, but we just don't know it yet. But you could say that if someone you trust saw a miracle, then you'd believe it. You would definitely believe it if it happened to you.

5 Miracles cause more problems for believers than they solve. Do you agree? Give reasons for your answer, showing you have thought about more than one point of view. (6 marks)

Grace's Answer

If God makes miracles happen, why does he make so few happen? If he was so powerful and loving, he'd help everyone instead of just one or two. This makes me think God isn't real, loving, or powerful – which makes God 'not God'!

But if I didn't believe in God and I got a miracle, I'd become a believer straight away. I think miracles help to make people believe – which is good for the religion, not bad.

Here's the commentary and tips for you to turn those answers into much better ones:

Answer 1 The explanation is weak, so could be clearer. Needs at least one example because the question asks for that.

Answer 2 Could be clearer. Needs another argument that is explained.

Answer 3 A very good outline of one quality of God, but to get 4 marks it needs to mention another couple as well.

Answer 4 Starts well, though only a little development. Then it goes on about why you'd believe in miracles – not the question, unfortunately.

Answer 5 This gives two sides, but there aren't enough reasons on either side, and not enough development either.

Topic Six Science and religion

This is the final topic in the course. It is split into three clear parts:

1 How science and religion differ and how they are similar.

2 The origins of the universe, including how humans' ideas about the world changed in the Middle Ages leading to a crisis in the Church.

3 The origins and development of life, including how that caused more upset in the Church. You will have met some of this in your science classes, so use this knowledge to help you in this subject (and this in that one!).

What is truth?

Go on, have a go at explaining what we mean by truth.

I think you should be able to get married at 16 if you want.

I am 16 and was born in Gloucester.

I'm allergic to chocolate! They did tests to prove it.

My mum and dad died when I was seven; I was adopted by my gran.

I like Italian food best.

I'll be a dancer; it's my favourite subject at school.

Abortion should be available to women – that's not saying it is good, because you can't just end a life.

I go to church on Sundays because I believe Christianity is the true faith.

I believe all our rules come from one ultimate source in the end.

This is Cherise. She's telling you some true things about herself. Do a diagram of yourself like the one above. There must be lots of things you can say about yourself.

Look at Cherise's comments. Are they all true? How do we define *truth*? What sorts of *truth* does Cherise use here? What sorts of *truth* have you used about yourself? Do you think they'll still be truths in five years? What does this tell you about *truth*?

Research Task

Find a dictionary definition of 'truth'. Find out as many different kinds of truth as you can. For each one, find an example.

Now you have thought about truth

Scientific truth versus religious truth

This course is particularly interested in two kinds of truth – **scientific truth** and **religious truth**: what they are; examples of them; how we get them; whether they clash or are compatible; and whether society likes one better than the other.

Scientific truth

Comes from *making a hypothesis*, then *testing* it to see if it is true. Seeing something happen again and again is important. This is called *repeated observation*. Think about how you do your coursework experiments in science – you write what you are trying to do, and what you think will happen. Then you do a lot of testing to check if you are right. Your tests confirm or disprove your idea.

It's things like $E = mc^2$, or that the Earth is in orbit around the Sun, or that the Northern Lights are a reflection of space dust hitting the atmosphere. In other words, scientific truth is describing our world and how it works.

Science answers the *what* and *how* questions – function and process.

Science is always open to change as we find out more information, or find out new circumstances. It isn't fixed; isn't absolute. It is always conditional, that is, true when based on the conditions in which testing/observation took place.

Religious truth

This comes from religions and holy books. We read it, are taught it or, for some people, they are told it by God. Many religions, or versions of a religion, are based on a person's experience of God.

It's things like explaining why we are here, who God is, how we should behave, and what will happen after we die. In other words, it gives us answers to **ultimate questions** – the questions no one else has an answer for, and which are really important to humans.

Religion answers the *why* questions – purpose and meaning.

Religion and holy books can be open to interpretation, but their words don't change. The truth of religion is considered to be *absolute* – unchanging and relevant for all time.

The Basics

1　What do we mean by 'scientific truth'? How is it found?
2　What do we mean by 'religious truth'? How is it found?
3　What similarities are there between scientific and religious truth?
4　What differences are there between scientific and religious truth?
5　Which kind of truth is more important? Explain why.

The origins of the universe

This is one of the areas in which it seems that science and religion disagree. You need to know what each side says, and also whether they can agree or not – in other words, are they *compatible* or *conflicting* kinds of truth?

The Big Bang Theory

> What is the evidence behind this scientific theory? What makes people believe it as a truth?

Scientists say the universe began about 20 billion years ago. There was nothing. Then there was a huge explosion. The explosion made a cloud of dust and gas. It took a long time for the universe to form into what we know of it today – the Sun, stars, planets and the universe itself.

What is the evidence? Well, an explosion causes everything to be flung outwards. There is no gravity in space, which means anything moving continues to move in the same direction at the same speed until another object acts on it (by hitting it, or being hit by it). Scientists know that the universe is still expanding, and that the movement can all be tracked back to a single point. This supports the idea of an explosion – it is as if the explosion is still being felt.

Another bit of evidence is what we call *background microwave radiation*. Explosions cause radiation and this can still be detected in space.

This was not the first theory of how the universe came to be. As scientists find new evidence, they reshape their ideas. In the case of the Big Bang, it replaced the Steady State Theory as the accepted view of the origins of the universe. There might be another theory waiting in the wings for that extra bit of persuasive evidence – such as the Pulsation Hypothesis Theory! That is one of the 'problems' of scientific theory and truth – it's open to change, development and revision. We could say that science is an evolving, changing description of the world and its workings – the truth for the time we are in with the knowledge we have.

Research Task

Find out more about the Big Bang Theory. Who thought of it? What is the evidence for it? Is it still considered to be the best explanation of how the universe began?

The Genesis creation story

A **creation** story is a story telling us how God created the world and universe.

The Christian creation story is written down in the Bible (Christian holy book). The first book of the Bible is called **Genesis**, which means 'beginning', and it begins with God's creation of the world.

This creation story is known as the Genesis creation story, or the Christian creation story, or the seven days of creation story. It is also believed by Jewish and Muslim people. You might already know it.

In Genesis, it says that at the beginning there was nothing. God decided to create the world. On each day of this creation, he made a new thing. On the first day, God created light. God separated light from dark, so that there was day and night. On the second day, God created the heavens. On the third day, God collected the water together to give land and sea. God also made plants of every kind grow on the land. On the fourth day, God created the sun, moon and stars, so that there were lights for the day and the night, and to mark the seasons. On the fifth day, God created the fish and birds. On the sixth day, God created animals, and then humans. Finally, on the seventh day, God rested. Each day, God had looked back at the creation and said that it was good. God had created a good world.

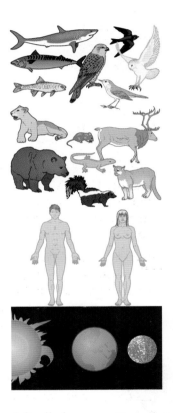

That creation story is understood in different ways. No matter how it is interpreted or understood, it is what we call a religious truth. Religious truth doesn't change; it is a truth for all time. Religious people believe that this is because it is a truth which came from God. God is eternal and without fault, so it must be true.

For some, it is literally true – word-for-word true. They believe in an all-loving, all-powerful and all-knowing God – so it isn't a problem to believe that God really could do this in the way described.

To many, the order of the creation makes sense – the planet, then the vegetation, then the fish and birds, then the animals, and finally humans. Genesis perhaps seems a little quick in comparison to what science says, but it was a story first told thousands of years ago – we can give the teller some leeway here. It is told in the only way it could be told, using the language and knowledge of the time.

When you think carefully about this story, there are some key messages in it. It is telling us that humans have a purpose – they were deliberately made by the creator, not an accident. It tells us this was a designed and considered creation – not just an accidental, chaotic happening. We are special in this story – and that is always good for our sense of well-being.

Now you know about origins of the universe

Science or religion, or both?

> Can you believe **both** science and religion on the matter of the origins of life? Read each of these people's understanding of Genesis. Which of them could believe in both Genesis and the Big Bang?

Josh believes that the Bible is the Word of God. Everything written in it is absolutely true. God told people exactly what to write. This includes Genesis. So Josh believes that every word in Genesis is true. He believes that the Genesis story is exactly how the world began. It is word-for-word true. The world was created in seven days by God.

Josh says that God can do anything and God is really clever. This means that God could create the world. Josh says that we will never understand how because we are humans not gods, so we should just believe it.

Ronnie believes that the Bible is true, but not word for word. He believes that God told people things, but they made some mistakes when they wrote them down. So the story in Genesis is right, but not exactly. For example, the story you have read uses the word 'days', but the original language uses a word that means 'periods of time'. Maybe the story was really saying that, over a long time, God made the world change and develop. Ronnie believes this. Ronnie believes that Genesis is more-or-less what happened.

Brett believes that the Bible is people's ideas about things that happened. He thinks that people thought about events and believed that God had been involved. This means that someone was saying how they believed the world began because of God. This means Genesis isn't word for word true. Brett still believes that God created the world. Scientists didn't exist when the story was first told. People had to tell the story in the way that made sense. Genesis makes sense, and it matches the way that scientists say the universe was formed and life developed.

The answer to who could believe in both Genesis and the Big Bang lies in how strictly they follow their religious story. Since it obviously isn't what the Big Bang says, then any literal understanding of Genesis is a problem. The two ideas don't say the same thing. However, the less literally we take Genesis, the easier it is to see it as a non-scientific way of understanding the world around us. If we think of Genesis as having a message for us, then it isn't even answering the same question as science – science is telling us *how*, whilst religion is telling us *why*.

It is the same with scientists though – the more strictly you believe that theory, the less room there is to believe anything else.

And, anyway, who made the Big Bang go bang?!

Now you know about interpreting stories

Comparing these truths

Which is more important – science or religion? If you look at the number of faith schools compared to the number of science schools, you might think religion was more important. If you compare how much time science takes up on your timetable with how much RE does, you might get a different answer. How many science programmes are on TV, compared to religious programmes? What about in the news – is there more science or more religion? Does either dominate news as a whole – or does it all depend on what is happening in the world at the time?

Science – as you have learned – is about hypotheses and testing; it describes observed regularities in the world around us; it helps us to make sense of how the world works. Religion is about giving a sense of purpose and meaning to our lives; it can act as a control because of its rules and the promise of an afterlife; it gives people a sense of well-being and comfort. *Are these things the same?*

Maybe the argument between science and religion needn't be there – because they are actually different kinds of truth, and so tell us different things. People will quite happily say that religion tells us things with no proof – just faith. Does science do the same when it gives us theories? The Big Bang is evidenced, not proven – but many believe it.

> *With a partner, try to work out why society seems to favour science over religion?*

You might have said science because it has proved lots of religious ideas wrong. Or because we live in a modern world. Or because religion isn't relevant today. Or that science has greater logic – so is more attractive.

> *Why does religion still prove strong in the world?*

You might have said religion because it answers questions nothing else can. Or it makes us feel special. Or it's a tradition. Or simply that it is right.

In our society, science holds a high place. It is very important to society's development and improvement right now, and it seems to have overtaken religion for many people. Science does challenge religious beliefs, and this course wants you to explore two of the biggest challenges science made. Over the next few pages, we will explore the cosmological revolution, and **evolution**.

The Basics

1 Explain what we mean by 'science' and 'religion'.
2 How do we find scientific truth, and how do we find religious truth?
3 Which is more important? Why?
4 **Both science and religion are valuable in our world today**. Do you agree? Give reasons and explain your answer, showing you have thought about more than one point of view.

The cosmological revolution

In the Middle Ages, our idea about what the world looked like was quite different to what we now know. The **cosmological revolution** is the term used to describe the change from the medieval view to the modern view. Let's start by looking at what medieval people thought the world was like – and why they thought this.

Our world

We believe that the world is a flat disc. The sky (firmament) is fixed in place like a dome. The Sun, Moon and stars move around the Earth. The Earth is held up on huge pillars, and the souls of the dead await inside the bowels of the Earth. Have a look at the picture – you will see what we mean.

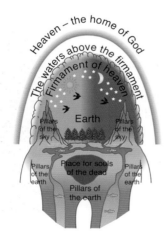

Why did they believe this?

Well, two main reasons: one, what they could see; two, what they were told from the Bible. If we know both, it helps us to understand because otherwise we might just think they were stupid or something! Why is their idea so different to ours? You have your experience, and so did medieval people. You also have the word and evidence of scientists – medieval people had theologians, religious men who took their truths from the Bible. This is a crucial difference.

What could they see?

If you go and stand in a field, what shape is the land? What shape is the sky? Is the world moving, or is it the Sun and clouds?

The land looks flat and at its edges it touches the sky. The edges of the Earth look the same distance away all round – so it's a disc. There aren't any folds in the sky, so that must be a sphere. It must be a dome over the earth, like an upturned bowl. The clouds and Sun move, but not you. The Earth – with you on it – is central to the whole of creation.

You can believe what you have just read – or go and check for yourself, and then believe it!

What were they told?

The Bible is a big set of books – lots to read. Medieval people couldn't read – they relied on monks and priests to tell them what was called the Word of God. If they were God's words, they had to be right. In the Book of Isaiah, it says that God has placed the world on *pillars*. In Genesis, the *windows of heaven* are described as being opened to cause a great flood. In the Book of Joshua, we read that Joshua commanded the Sun to stop still – and it did. In the Book of Job, we are told that the dead are beneath the earth. These all helped to make that idea of the world.

The Basics

1 Describe the medieval idea of what the world looked like.
2 Explain why medieval people believed this.
3 Do you think it was reasonable for medieval people to believe this? Explain your answer.

Now you know the medieval world view

The voices of change

Several scientific people were key in changing the medieval world view. You could be asked about any of them. More likely, you will be asked to describe some of the major changes in the cosmological revolution, but it makes it clearer if you know those changes in context. Please note – many of these people were very religious, which goes against our idea that religion and science don't mix!

Nicolaus Copernicus

Copernicus was a Polish monk who lived from 1473 to 1543. He had studied maths and astronomy in Poland, then went to Italy to further his studies, and finally studied medicine. By 1506, Copernicus was becoming known as an astronomer of some merit, and was beginning to publish on the subject.

His great contribution was to show that the world was not central to the universe – the Sun was. He took observations from others, and checked the logic of the ideas. Then he did the scientific thing, and went for the idea that was most straightforward and simplistic. He said it made most sense if the Sun was central to the universe, and the world and all other planets moved around the Sun. After all, you should always put the light in the middle for greatest effect, he reasoned – the Sun is the light for the universe, and God put it in the middle.

Tycho Brahe

The man with the golden nose! Brahe lost his nose in a duel and had a gold one screwed into his skull in its place. Brahe didn't spot anything, but he did make people look somewhere other than the Bible for their information. He made regular and detailed observations of the stars and planets throughout his life. This led him to publish what is regarded as being the most accurate set of star tables. This gave astronomers new accurate information to use. It also encouraged others to look at the stars for themselves.

Johannes Kepler

Kepler lived from 1571 to 1630. Brahe had offered him a job but he never took it. He was a mathematician who lived in Prague, but he used his maths to try to work out how the planets moved. Copernicus had said the planets move around the Sun, but still in circles. Kepler used maths to prove that the movement of the planets was actually elliptical (egg-shaped). He also proved that the Sun wasn't in the middle – it was at one of the ends of the ellipse.

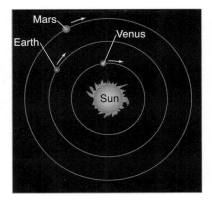

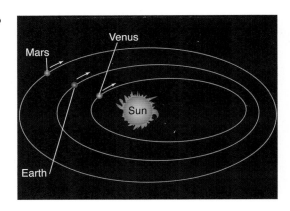

Galileo Galilei

Galileo (1564–1642) is one of the most famous scientists of all time. In fact, he was a mathematician, but he used maths to work out what he could see when he looked at the stars. He applied mathematical reasoning and principles to astronomy. So, now you know maths isn't just about crunching numbers!

Galileo heard about the first telescope – which had been made in Amsterdam. He used maths to work out how to make one for himself, and then made one. He used it to observe the stars. Before this, people had relied on only what they could see with the naked eye – which isn't much actually! Galileo was able to make more detailed star charts than ever before, which he published across Europe so that all scholars could have access to this new information. He also established the practice of observation rather than relying on scripture for answers to scientific questions.

In his observations, Galileo saw that the Moon was not a perfect sphere – as was previously believed. It had mountains and valleys, craters and plains. It was an imperfect object in what was believed to be a perfect heaven. He also saw that Venus had shadows across it that differed through the month. This suggested Venus did not move around the Earth, but around the Sun – strengthening the Copernican Sun-centred view of the universe. Galileo was also able to see that Jupiter had its own moons that orbited around it.

Challenging religion

Galileo's observations proved a direct challenge to the Church because they proved the Church wrong. It was no longer possible to believe that the heavens (anything outside the Earth's firmament) were perfect. It was no longer possible to believe the Earth was the centre of the creation. The creation was seen to be much bigger and more complex than anything previously imagined. More importantly, those Bible passages that had described the world were simply wrong as scientific facts.

The Church's response was to summon Galileo before the Inquisition. This was a committee that had the power to excommunicate people. In Galileo's day, to be excommunicated meant to be cut off from God's world. It would be impossible for his soul to enter heaven. People really believed this – it was a very powerful threat. Galileo was forced to renounce everything he had said and published, and lived the rest of his life in exile (though he didn't get excommunicated, which was a huge relief!)

The Basics

1 Who was Galileo?
2 What did Galileo do to give accurate star details to the rest of Europe?
3 What significant observations were made by Galileo?
4 How did these challenge the Church?
5 **Galileo started modern science**. What do you think? Explain your opinion.

Now you know about Galileo

Sir Isaac Newton

Sir Isaac Newton (1643–1727) was British. He is considered to be the 'father' of modern science – so great was his contribution. Galileo had made scientists look and learn, instead of just accepting what they were told. Newton wrote the rule book for scientists of the future.

Newton tidied up the ideas that had come before him. He put them together into a meaningful and understandable structure. Most people know of Newton because of the story of the apple, which he watched fall. Johannes Kepler came up with three laws of motion and Newton studied Kepler's work. Newton realised that there must be a force that controls or affects motion. From this realisation came his law of gravitation, and this made Kepler's laws make sense – other people could see their truth because of Newton.

Perhaps Newton's greatest contribution – and the reason he is so highly regarded – was that he set up a system of principles that science would operate by. There were four rules in this.

Rules of science

1 It is wrong to bring God into an event that can be adequately explained without him.

2 The same events have the same causes. In other words, nature operates through regular systems.

3 What is true for one thing is true for all – we can't say the planets are in heaven, so have different operating rules; everything is part of the same system.

4 Science is a description of what is observed. Scientific truth is made through hypothesis, testing and observation.

The key to all of Newton's system is that we should rely on science (as in Rule 4) and not on scripture for our answers to how the world (and universe) works.

No God?!

Does all this mean Newton was doing away with God?

Actually, no, it doesn't. As well as being the 'father' of science and the first of the modern scientists, Newton was probably the last to attribute everything to God. He saw the world and universe as a kind of machine, which ran because of systems and processes. He believed that God had designed the universe, and that it was designed in such a way as to keep going, correcting any problems if they came up. The laws of nature that Newton claimed the world ran on were actually laws set up by God to ensure his creation's smooth running.

This was a huge 'wow' factor – God could be seen as an even more amazing creator and intelligent designer. Just think – what kind of intellect could produce a machine as vast and complicated as the universe, with built-in maintenance systems? Wow!

The Basics

1 Who was Sir Isaac Newton?
2 What was Newton's contribution to science?
3 Explain how Newton excluded God from scientific discovery.
4 Explain how Newton understood God to be crucial to scientific discovery.
5 **Newton was the most important figure in the cosmological revolution.** What do you think? Explain your opinion.

Now you know about Newton

Key points of the cosmological revolution

Let's have a look at the difference those men on pages 77–9 made to scientific thinking, and how it changed the world view. You will also spot some of the reasons why the Church felt challenged by this changing thinking.

Before this person	Scientist	Their 'discovery'
Belief that the world was central to the creation. Everything moved around the Earth. Heavens were perfect.	Copernicus	Sun-centred universe, with the Earth moving around the Sun.
People accepted what the Bible told them. They used this to help them explain what they could see in nature.	Brahe	He made people do their own observations – find out for themselves.
The belief was that the planets moved in circles in the heavens.	Kepler	Showed that the motion was elliptical.
People believed that the heavenly bodies (planets, Sun, etc.) were perfect spheres. That the heavens were where God was, so had to be infallible. Also people still depended on the biblical teachings for answers.	Galileo	Established the practice of observation to find answers. He also saw that the heavenly bodies were neither perfect nor spherical. He also proved the Sun-centred view.
Science relied on God as an answer to problems. It saw the heavens as having its own set of rules.	Newton	He set up a set of rules for science, which excluded God. He explained why Kepler's laws of motion were true. He laid the foundations of science.

From this:

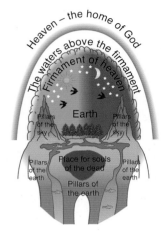

To this:

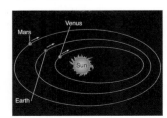

This whole change of thinking, and change in understanding of what the universe was like was a huge challenge to the Church. The Church had controlled learning for centuries in Europe, and had basically written the rules. These scientists challenged what the Church had said were truths given by God. It was a bit like a row of dominoes – push one and they all fall. If one bit of Church teaching was wrong, how much more was wrong? The Church could see its authority and, from that, its power being lessened.

Now you know how the world view changed

The next big clash...evolution

So, the Church (essentially the Roman Catholic Church) was challenged by the changing world view, but got over it. Today, there are many scientists who live and work within the Roman Catholic tradition, even in the Vatican.

The next really huge challenge was brought by Charles Darwin's theory of evolution. This theory tried to explain how life had developed into what we see today.

Before Darwin

Before Darwin, people believed that humans were exactly as God had created them. In fact, the world was as it had been created. Now any of you who have studied geography know that the weather changes the world – it wears away rocks, for example. The continents are not as they were millions of years ago, because they sit on enormous plates that slide, collide and move. Mountains are examples of where these plates have collided, and kept moving together. New islands are created by volcanoes under the ocean. You know this, but people in the eighteenth century didn't. They truly believed that the world was as God created it. Why did they believe this? Because

Before Darwin people believed that the world was the same as it always had been

the Church said so. What the Church said came from God – so it was true.

The Bible was still regarded as an absolute truth. The creation stories in Genesis were believed true – God had made the world in seven days. In the sixteenth century, Archbishop Ussher had worked out the date the earth was created. He worked out how long ago Jesus had lived, then used the family trees found in the New and Old Testaments to count the number of generations between Jesus and Adam. Giving each generation a number of years, he came up with 4004 BCE. The world was just 6000 years old! This was accepted as true.

'What about the fossils?' I hear you say! Well, they said that God had created fossils with the appearance of age – as a test of man's faith. No one knew about things like carbon-dating and other tests to determine age, so they just accepted the idea. It fitted with their existing beliefs.

Scholars had begun to suggest that the world changed. There were some theories about animals changing and developing; Lyell in the 1830s wrote a book about geology. In fact, the earliest evolution-style theory was written by Thales (a Greek) in 550 BCE. However, nothing had the impact that Darwin's ideas had.

The Victorian period was a really insecure time for religion in Britain. People were serious about their religion, but the faith they had was quite shaky. It was a time ripe for trouble! And along came Darwin!

Research Task

Find out the theories of the following people:

- Thales
- Linnaeus
- Charles Lyell.

Show how their ideas could have contributed to the idea of an changing/evolving world and nature.

Charles Darwin and evolution

Charles Darwin was a natural scientist. He wrote a book called *On the Origin of Species*, published in 1859. This was the culmination of years of research including travels on the scientific exploration ship, *HMS Beagle*.

In *On the Origin of Species*, Darwin suggested that the world is a place of change, and that the huge variety of creatures and species is the result of thousands of years of change and adaptation. He said that there is a struggle for survival between species. Where species failed to adapt, they became extinct, so that only the fittest (best-suited) could survive. He called this **natural selection**. Darwin also realised that different places caused different species of the same creature, because the places made different demands on the creatures. For example, birds had different shaped beaks depending on whether they lived in an area where berries were abundant, or in an area where shellfish were the main food.

Let's try and explain this in a different way, which should make it easier for you to grasp.

Look around you at the world and everything in it. Do things change? Do people change? Is there anything that doesn't change?

When you came to secondary school, it was a big change from life at primary school. If you have moved from one secondary school to another, that's a big change too. How did you cope with the difference? Do different people cope in different ways?

If you went to live in a very cold country, things would be very different for you. You would have to make changes to your life. What would happen if you didn't?

These are the main elements of evolutionary theory. When we look at the world around us, we can see many, many different varieties of animals, birds, fish, insects and people. For example, birds with different types of beaks.

If we look at the environment in which these animals live, we can see there are great differences. For

example, some places are much hotter than others. Environments are always changing; volcanoes may erupt covering the surrounding area with ash, altering the shape of the landscape.

We can also see that the creatures in an area are suited to that particular environment. A polar bear has special fur, which makes it possible for it to live in cold temperatures.

Many scientists believe that the world has always been changing. Creatures have had to get used to the change and adapt to it, or they have died. Where a whole species could not adapt, it has become extinct. Where a species did adapt, its biology has changed so that the species survived.

This theory suggests that nothing was designed to look like it does today, or to work in the way it does today. Things have changed in order to survive, so the idea of design must be wrong. So is the idea that the world is as it has always been. Those Victorian ideas were being challenged.

Now you know about evolution

No God?

You'd think that this evolution theory completely discarded God. No longer could people claim the world was the same perfect creation of God. The idea of the seven-day creation was also challenged. So, was it time to pension God off? Was science finally getting rid of God?

Well, Darwin still claimed God was involved in all of this. In the final chapter of *On the Origin of Species*, Darwin asks where all the intelligence within nature, and the complexity and interdependence came from. He finds it difficult to believe that without some sort of guidance, there isn't just total chaos. He puts it down to God – God created the original life-forms with the ability to adapt and change. It isn't design down to the fine detail; it is design via intelligence and adaptability.

Now, God is even greater than was first thought – his creations adapt and change.

So why the trouble?

There was a lot of trouble over Darwin's theory. In Topic One, you met William Paley's design argument (page 4). His argument was that the creation proved God existed because everything had been created with a purpose. This was not what Darwin was saying – he was saying things had changed and evolved. His theory disputed the belief in God's complete and perfect creation. Just as the cosmological revolution had challenged the very authority of the Church, Darwin's theory was seen as a challenge to belief in God itself.

The evolution theory also suggested that humans were descended from apes. Victorian England had just seen an exhibition of stuffed gorillas, all in fierce poses. This exhibition was managed by Paul Belloni du Chaillu, and he took great pleasure in telling tales of how fierce and savage the gorillas were in the wild. People didn't like the idea of these creatures being their ancestors – far too uncivilised! It didn't make them want to believe Darwin.

So that's where your mother got her looks

A famous test for the new theory came in 1860 at the British Association for the Advancement of Science in Oxford. Darwin's friend, Huxley, was forced to debate the theory with Bishop Wilberforce. There is no complete record of what exactly was said, but there are reports. Famously, Wilberforce asked Huxley on which side he was related to apes – his father's or mother's! The result was that science and religion were in complete opposition.

Research Task

Find out about Darwin's background, and then find out about his travels. Present your information as a word-processed report.

The Basics

1 Who was Darwin?
2 Explain Darwin's theory of evolution.
3 How did Darwin include God in his theory?
4 Why did Darwin's theory challenge religion?
5 **Evolution gets rid of the need for God.** What do you think? Explain your opinion.

Now you know how evolution challenged religion

Science versus religion

The exam could ask you whether science and religion agree or disagree, whether they are compatible or contradictory. You need to be able to argue this using creation and/or evolution as a focus. So let's have a look at both.

> With a partner, make a list of how science and religion agree, and how they disagree.
> Next, make a list of how science and religion agree and disagree when it comes to the start of the universe.
> Finally, make a list of how science can agree and disagree when it comes to the origins of life.

You may find that you kept coming up with the same answers, or that the same answers fitted more than one of those lists. That is fine, because these lists aren't exclusive, and the examiner can't ask you more than one of those questions in the exam.

Are science and religion compatible?

Use these statements to build a two-sided argument to answer this question. You can add your own ideas as well.

- Religion has God; science explains God away.
- Religion explains *why* (the start); science explains *how* (the process).
- Science builds facts; religion relies on faith.
- Science works out answers; religion just puts God in the gap.

Can we believe in both science and religion concerning the beginning of the universe?

Use these statements, and your own, to build a two-sided argument to answer this question. You have to explain the points.

- The creation story says it took seven days; science says it took billions of years.
- Both the creation story and the Big Bang begin with light.
- Scientists can't explain what made the Big Bang happen; religious believers of the Big Bang say it was God.
- Big Bang has no God; the religious version is about God.

Can we believe in both science and religion concerning the origins of life?

Use these statements, and your own, to build a two-sided argument to answer this question. Don't forget to explain the points.

- The creation story says it took seven days; science says it took billions of years.
- Evolution could have been God's design.
- The creation story mentions no species, and certainly doesn't mention the dinosaurs; science proves many species and dinosaurs.
- Science can explain the origins of life, without God.

Created or evolved – what difference does it make?

> *What difference does it make to a person's attitude if they were created rather than evolved?*

Is this a stupid question? Or just one you have never thought of the implications of?!

 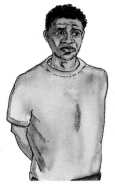 

If you were told that your conception and existence were planned, that your mum and dad thought about making and then having a baby, that they planned your room and how they'd bring you up, that you were central to their life and dreams, how would this make you feel? Would you feel really special and loved? Would it make you feel really good about yourself?

What if you were told you were a complete accident? Neither intended nor really wanted – you just happened. Once you were in existence, the situation was accepted, and your parents got on with life. They reshaped their life to include you. They love you – you are a product of them, so they have a natural attachment to you. Now how do you feel? Good or bad? Special or not?

The first description really is what Genesis and the creation story are about. They give meaning and purpose to human existence. They make us feel special, and that we have a special place in the universe.

The second description is what evolution is about – accidents and adaptations. Nothing special, nothing planned.

The religious stories of how the world and life began make humans see life in a different context. They can affect people's attitude to life and to each other. If we believe life is special, then it must be protected and cherished.

The scientific theories make the world more hostile because it is impersonal. If everything is down to science – the survival of the fittest, and adaptation to environment – then we have no motivation to be good or moral. We just have to survive.

> *So, what do you think? Do you prefer science or religion? Why?*

 Now you have thought about how beliefs shape attitude

85

Exam tips – building your technique

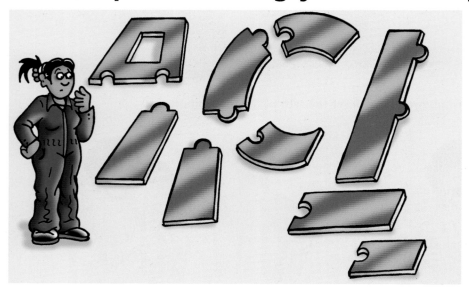

Let's start with a bunch of questions, and use them for each task on this page.

1 Explain what is meant by the Big Bang.

2 Explain what is meant by evolution.

3 Explain what is meant by religious truth and scientific truth.

4 What is the difference between religious truth and scientific truth?

5 In your own words, write one creation story.

6 Is it possible to believe in science and religion regarding the beginning of the universe?

7 Explain the most important changes during the cosmological revolution.

8 How did science challenge religion in either the cosmological revolution or the evolution debate?

Getting to an F grade

Actually, it is quite easy to make an F grade. Your teacher must have told you that you should try to answer every question – even if you are guessing. They are right – you don't lose marks for getting anything wrong. The worst that could happen is that the examiner gets a laugh out of it!

So, you need to be able to give one correct answer to every question or, if you can, a couple of correct answers – just in case some are wrong.

Try to give one answer to each of those questions. Remember it has to be relevant and correct to get the mark.

So, if you did that all through the paper, you'd walk an 'F' grade. But you don't just want that, do you? So let's look at building on that F, and getting the C.

Getting to a C grade

If you just had to get 1 mark per question to get an F, now you'll have to get 2 marks to get a C. You will have to give two different and correct ideas in each answer.

A word to the boys! Boys are really good at writing the first thing that comes into their head, and then moving on to the next question. For a lot of boys, just waiting and thinking is a hard habit to learn – but you have to do it. As an examiner, the author of this book sees this all the time – and your teacher will back this up. So, get into the habit of giving two answers. Crack that habit, and then you'll be ready to make your move on the highest grades.

If the topics on the paper are split into five parts (as AQA recommends to principal examiners), 2 marks for every part means you'll accumulate about 40 marks across the paper. The paper is out of 72, so this will be enough for a C grade, and could well be enough for a B.

Okay, try to give two answers to each of the questions. It's okay to reuse the answers you used earlier – but you'll feel even cleverer if you can come up with two new ones!

Getting to an A grade

It isn't quite as easy to get the A grade. Sorry, that was a bit obvious, wasn't it?! The thing is, to get an A grade, you can't just give relevant answers. You have to explain yourself. We're talking about showing that you can develop ideas, that you can evaluate comments and make judgements. They are quite tough skills. However, you can train yourself to do a bit more with your answer, and so improve it. If you can grab 3 of every 4 marks available, you *will* get that A grade.

Here's the technique: when you have given your two answers (for the C grade – remember), explain one of them by developing the point and providing an example to show what you mean. Or explain both of the points.

You have got some answers to work with – either two or three for each – so use them to practise the A-grade building.

You can do this for any of the topics, and you need to really, so that you get good practice using the techniques. Lots of practice means you will do it without even thinking about what you are doing – it becomes the way you write. Now that isn't just good for this subject – it helps to build marks in all of your subjects.

ABERDEENSHIRE
BANCHORY ACADEMY
COUNCIL

Appendix 1

Revision outline

This is a revision guide. It follows the outline of topics in the specification. If you already know all of the answers when you read through it, you will probably do brilliantly.

Use the guide as a checklist of what you know, and what you have still got to get to grips with. You could even use it as a last-minute check before you go into the exam. When you have finished all your revision, you should be able to recognise each word. Each phrase should trigger a whole lot of ideas in your head – linked people, examples and explanations. When it does, you are ready.

TOPIC	WORDS TO LEARN	SUBJECTS WITHIN TOPICS – DO YOU KNOW…?
ONE: THE EXISTENCE OF GOD	First Cause Design Evolution Miracle Religious experience Morality Proof	• Why people believe or don't believe in God • The First Cause argument for God's existence • The problems with this argument • The design argument • The problems with this argument • The argument from miracles • The problems with this argument • The argument from religious experience • The problems with this argument • The argument from morality • The problems with this argument • Arguments against God's existence • Which arguments are stronger or weaker, and why
TWO: REVELATION	Revelation Special revelation General revelation Worship Nature Holy books Prayer Nature of God Reality Illusion	• What the difference is between special and general revelation • Examples of special revelation • Examples of all types of general revelation • The relative strengths and weaknesses of special and general revelation • Whether revelation proves that God exists • What is meant by reality and illusion • Why some people say revelation is illusion • Why some people say revelation is real • What we learn about God through revelation • Problems caused by the idea of revelation

TOPIC	WORDS TO LEARN	SUBJECTS WITHIN TOPICS – DO YOU KNOW…?
THREE: THE PROBLEMS OF EVIL AND SUFFERING	Evil Moral evil Natural evil Suffering Theodicy Devil The Fall Benevolence Omnipotence Omniscience Eternal Test Education Punishment	• What is meant by evil? • What is meant by suffering? • Why moral evil causes problems for those believing in God • Why natural evil causes problems for those believing in God • How evil and suffering provide proof for some that God does not exist • How religious people defend God in regard to moral evil • How religious people defend God in regard to natural evil • How religious believers respond in the face of evil and suffering
FOUR: IMMORTALITY	Immortality Resurrection Reincarnation Rebirth Life after death Ghost Spiritualism Near-death experience Revelation Soul Dualism	• What is meant by immortality? • What could count as immortality – resurrection, reincarnation, rebirth, legacy, memories – and what these mean • The problems of each of these forms • What would live forever – body/spirit/mind/some/all? • The problems of each of these options • What evidence there is of immortality – ghosts, near-death experiences, spiritualism, scripture – and how these provide evidence • What evidence is there against immortality
FIVE: MIRACLES	Miracle Law of nature Nature of God	• What we mean by miracle • Examples of miracles • Evidence of miracles • What we learn about God through miracles • Hume's argument against miracles • Why people want miracles to happen • Problems caused by accepting events as miracles • How miracles help to strengthen belief in God

TOPIC	WORDS TO LEARN	SUBJECTS WITHIN TOPICS – DO YOU KNOW...?
SIX: SCIENCE AND RELIGION	Science Religion Truth Compatibility Big Bang Theory Genesis creation story Cosmological revolution Design Intelligent design Evolution	• What we mean by truth • How truth changes • What we mean by absolute and relative truth • Whether we can accept science and religion together • Whether science and religion answer the same questions in the same way • What the Big Bang Theory is • What Genesis says • How the current world view developed from the medieval view • How science has challenged religion over the origins of the universe • Whether the Big Bang Theory and Genesis are compatible • What the design argument says • What evolution says • Whether design and evolution are compatible • How evolutionary theory challenged religious belief • Whether belief in design/evolution affects our behaviour

Appendix II

Sample paper

What a question paper looks like

You will be given a question paper and an answer booklet in the examination.

> Do I really need to read the cover?
> It's always the same isn't it?

Well, no, they aren't all the same, and it is easy in a stressful situation to mix up what you are meant to do. Probably your teacher will have told you a million times what you have to do in the exam, but you can still forget. It is always a good idea to just check through the cover – it is like a calming exercise that helps if you are nervous. It also reassures you that you do know what you are doing.

The cover will remind you:

- how long the exam lasts – so plan and use your time well. Reassess after each full question answered – you might have gained or lost some time. Don't spend too much time on one question, but don't rush yourself either. You start with four questions to answer in 90 minutes – about 22 minutes a question.
- that you get a choice of any four of the six questions on offer. If you answer them all, you'll be given marks for the best four, but it might not be the best use of your time. Some people find they have lots of time left when they have finished what they should do, so they do extra questions to pass the time! Examiners don't recommend it!
- to use blue or black ink/pen. This makes your paper easier to read and mark. This is especially important when exam papers are going to be marked online. You need your writing to be clear and bold, so the examiner doesn't have to struggle to read it.
- that you should do any notes or practice work on either your answer booklet, or on extra paper. Sometimes, people write correct things that they then don't put into their real answer. If you hand in all your working out and notes, the examiner can credit you for anything you missed out. They are obliged to read it all. In your answer booklet, write on the lines only – don't go into the margins or above/below the box. The online mark reader (OMR) system that scans your booklet into the computer for the examiner to mark online isn't designed to pick up anything outside of the writing area – it might cost you marks.

So much for the cover, what about the inside?

There will be six questions and the chances are that each one will have a picture or bit of writing to start with. The pictures are meant to stimulate your brain and start you thinking. In other words, they are meant to help you by triggering the relevant ideas for that question.

In this sample paper, the marks in the questions are split 2/3/3/4/6. There has to be a 3 and a 6-mark evaluative question, but the other 9 marks could be split up in a different way – could be 1/2/6, 3/6 or 4/5, for example. So be prepared (through the practice in this book) for this.

There are six questions. You have to answer four. If you answer more, your best four will be used to work out your grade.

Answer any **four** questions

9 marks for knowledge-type questions.
9 marks for 'Do you agree?' type questions.

Each question is worth **18 marks**

1. The existence of God

The stimulus resource could be a picture, photo or text. It is meant to help you with the question.

(a) Give **two** reasons why some people do **not** believe in God. *(2 marks)*

Two reasons for 2 marks.

Don't say why they *do*.

(b) Explain briefly the First Cause argument for the existence of God. *(3 marks)*

Must say something and add more about that point.

Don't describe any other – Aquinas, right?

(c) 'Religious experiences are just illusions.'

What do you think? Explain your opinion. *(3 marks)*

Don't bother arguing against it.

(d) Explain why some people think the design argument can prove that God exists. *(4 marks)*

Stick to this argument for your answers.

This means they don't make people believe in God.

(e) 'None of the arguments for God's existence are convincing.'

Do you agree? Give reasons for your answer, showing you have thought about more than one point of view. *(6 marks)*

Two sides in this answer – agree and disagree

2.   Revelation

Read this account of someone's experience of God.

If you are told to read something, DO IT! It is meant to help you.

I sat in that room, and wept. My daughter lying in her coffin. Why did she have to die? She was too young. I felt as if my grief would consume me – so huge was my sorrow. Then from somewhere I felt as if I was being held. As if someone was trying to comfort me. And I felt as if I could go on with life.

This is describing a religious experience.

(a)   Give **two** ways in which people claim to have experienced God.   (*2 marks*)

It doesn't matter whether or not you believe them.

(b)   'Only fools think they can see God.'

What do you think? Explain your opinion.   (*3 marks*)

You can't get full marks if you don't give an example.

(c)   Using examples, explain briefly what is meant by special revelation.   (*3 marks*)

Direct revelation.

(d)   Explain what religious believers learn about God through revelation.   (*4 marks*)

Wants to know characteristics of God.

Key words. Is it better or not?

(e)   'General revelation is better proof of God than special revelation.'

Do you agree? Give reasons for your answer, showing you have thought about more than one point of view.   (*6 marks*)

3. **The problems of evil and suffering**

This stimulus helps with this question.

MAN CONVICTED OF MURDERING HIS FAMILY

LOCAL COUNCILLOR ENCOURAGES HATRED FOR ETHNIC MINORITIES IN COMMUNITY

HURRICANE IKE DESTROYS TOWNS IN CUBA

'NO NEARER TO A CURE FOR AIDS' SAY SCIENTISTS

(a) Explain briefly the difference between moral evil and natural evil. *(2 marks)*

(b) What problems are caused for religious believers by evil? *(3 marks)*

Key word.

Stick to moral (human made) evil in your answer.

(c) 'Moral evil is the work of the devil.'

What do you think? Explain your opinion. *(3 marks)*

Key word.

(d) Explain how religious believers have tried to explain why God allows evil and suffering. *(4 marks)*

(e) 'There is suffering because God does not care about his creation.'

Do you agree? Give reasons for your answer, showing you have thought about more than one point of view. *(6 marks)*

4. **Immortality**

Look at this picture. It shows orbs (light anomalies) around a famous old car.

(a) Give **two** pieces of evidence for immortality. (*2 marks*)

(b) Explain briefly what is meant by reincarnation. (*3 marks*)

(c) 'There is nothing good about living forever.'
What do you think? Explain your opinion. (*3 marks*)

Know this term.

(d) Explain the problems met in believing in the resurrection of the body. (*4 marks*)

Key word.

(e) 'There is no such thing as life after death.'
Do you agree? Give reasons for your answer, showing you have thought
about more than one point of view. (*6 marks*)

5. **Miracles**

   Read the statement below:

   > Doctors told me my son was dying of cancer. There was no cure.
   > They could only reduce his pain. I prayed. Then a miracle happened,
   > and my son's cancer disappeared. He is alive, well and happy – thanks
   > to God.

   (a) Why might they say that this event was a 'miracle'?   (*2 marks*)

   Use this stimulus – it has the answers.

   (b) If this event was a miracle, explain briefly what we can learn about God from it.   (*3 marks*)

   Characteristics of God.

   (c) 'Only God can make miracles happen.'

       What do you think? Explain your opinion.   (*3 marks*)

   (d) Explain some of the problems caused by saying this event is a miracle.   (*4 marks*)

   Key word.

   (e) 'Miracles are proof that God doesn't love us all.'

       Do you agree? Give reasons for your answer, showing you have thought about
       more than one point of view.   (*6 marks*)

   Must be two sides to your answer – agree and disagree.

6.   Science and religion

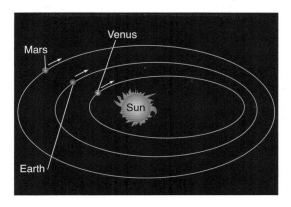

(a)   Explain the Big Bang Theory.   (*2 marks*)

(b)   'Evolution proves that God does not exist.'

What do you think? Explain your opinion.   (*3 marks*)

> Write about what two people said/did at this time.

(c)   (i) Explain **two** ways in which people's ideas about the world changed in the cosmological revolution.   (*4 marks*)

(ii) Explain briefly why this was a problem for the Church at the time.   (*3 marks*)

> Means 'challenge to its authority'.

(d)   'It is impossible to believe in both scientific truth and religious truth.'

Do you agree? Give reasons for your answer, showing you have thought about more than one point of view.   (*6 marks*)

> Use truth generally, but also refer to the Big Bang and evolution for examples for/against the statement.

Glossary

Agnostic a person who believes there are reasons for and against God's existence, hence, remain unsure or open-minded

All-knowing (omniscient) a term used to describe God – that he knows everything it is possible to know; God's intelligence is unlimited

All-loving (benevolent) term used to describe God – that he loves each of us as individuals; God's love is unlimited

All-powerful (omnipotent) term used to describe God – that he is as powerful as it is possible to be: includes the ability to create the world; God's power is unlimited

Anatta 'not soul', the combination of elements (skandhas) such as emotions and intelligence which makes each person unique and individual. These are always changing, and so there is 'no soul', though this ever-changing combination is the link between many lifetimes.

Atheist a person who believes God does not exist

Atman soul that will be reborn into many lifetimes

BCE Before common era. Used instead of BC by non-Christians.

Belief what someone accepts as being true for them

Bible holy book of Christianity

Big Bang Theory scientific theory about the origins of the universe

CE Common era. Used instead of AD by non-Christians.

Charles Darwin (1809–1862) author of *On the Origin of Species* (1859), which discussed ideas of evolution

Cosmological revolution the change in understanding of the layout of the universe

Creation religious explanations of how the universe came about, how God made the world; Genesis creation story

Design a preliminary plan or idea for something to be established

Devil/Satan the supreme spirit of evil

Dualism idea that mind and body are completely distinct elements that make up a human

Enlightenment breaking free from cycle of reincarnation/rebirth

Eternal everlasting, never-ending

Evolution theory of development of life from simple to complex forms

First Cause argument to prove the existence of God, based on God as First Cause of the world; St Thomas Aquinas

General revelation indirect experience of God, where a person sees something of God through something else, e.g. through the work of good people

Genesis first book of the Bible or Torah; here we mean the story of how God created the world in seven days, a story shared by Christians and Jews

Illusion a false belief; something wrongly believed to exist; deceptive appearances; 'all in the mind'

Immanent God is involved in his creation, e.g. in the person of Christ in the world

Immanuel Kant (1724–1804) a German philosopher who wrote the argument from morality

Immortality live forever, never die; eternal life

Impersonal meaning that people cannot relate to God personally

Infallible not capable of being wrong. Religions believe God is infallible.

Laws of nature how nature works, assuming it follows certain principles, e.g. day always follows night

Life after death life after the death of the body in this lifetime

Medium a person who has psychic abilities and can communicate with the souls of the dead

Miracle an event that is contradictory to the normal order of things; impossible – usually applied to an action of God, and is always good

Moral evil the pain caused by the words and actions of humans

Moral truth truth established through morality, based on ideas of right and wrong

Morality the sense of right and wrong

Natural evil pain caused by the activities of nature, e.g. because of an earthquake

Natural selection survival of the fittest amongst species – those that adapt to the changing environment survive; those that don't adapt become extinct

Near-death experience an experience whereby someone believes they have died, but their consciousness has continued and they have met dead people who they knew when alive or religious figures

On the Origin of Species book written by Charles Darwin (1859) regarding evolution

Paradise a state of complete bliss often used as a reference to God's Garden of Eden

Personal relating to God described in human terms – he listens, speaks, cares, knows, etc.

Proof a fact or thing that helps to show the truth

Reality what is real or actually exists

Rebirth the belief that our ever-changing self will be reborn into many lifetimes in a search for enlightenment

Reincarnation the belief that our soul will be reincarnated many times to live many lifetimes in a search for enlightenment

Religious experience an experience that leaves one feeling one has met God in some way

Religious truth truth established from religion, e.g. from holy books

Resurrection idea that each person will be physically brought back to life at the Day of Judgement

Revelation when God reveals himself to humans

Saul in the New Testament, he was a Jew who became a Christian known as Paul

Scientific truth truths established by science, through observed regularity and testing of hypotheses

Soul non-physical part of a human, which is thought to continue after the death of the body, e.g. going to heaven

Special revelation direct revelation of God, e.g. meeting God

Spiritual truth truth established through religion and spirituality, often giving answers to ultimate questions

Spiritualism religious belief that disembodied spirits of the dead surviving in another world/dimension can make contact with the living in this world, especially through mediums

St Thomas Aquinas (1225–74CE) monk and theologian; wrote the First Cause argument

Teleological argument argument to prove God's existence through evidence of design in the world

The Fall the story of how Adam and Eve were cast out of the Garden of Eden, and how evil and suffering came into the creation as a result of their actions

Theist a person who believes that God exists

Theodicy defence of God against accusations, e.g. why he allows evil and suffering to exist when this is clearly not compatible with the idea of a loving, powerful and intelligent God

Transcendent in relation to God, beyond space and time – limitless

Ultimate questions questions for which science has no answers, such as why are we here? What happens after we die? Does God exist?

Ultimate Reality Hindu idea of God, Brahman

Undeserved something that happens to a person which is not just or right

William Paley (1743–1805) put forward a teleological argument for the existence of God

Index

Index